Voyage of the Skylands: Island of Ascension

Voyage of the Skylands, Volume 2

Linus Running

Published by Linus Running, 2024.

While every precaution has been taken in the preparation of this book, the publisher assumes no responsibility for errors or omissions, or for damages resulting from the use of the information contained herein.

VOYAGE OF THE SKYLANDS: ISLAND OF ASCENSION

First edition. September 23, 2024.

Copyright © 2024 Linus Running.

ISBN: 979-8227841964

Written by Linus Running.

The winds were calm as the crew sailed through the open skies. The atmosphere was lighter, with the recent battles behind them, but a sense of anticipation filled the air. Kaida leaned over the edge of the ship, her eyes scanning the horizon. "So where are we headed next?" she asked, her voice casual, but curiosity danced in her tone.

Ryu stood at the helm, arms crossed as he stared into the distance. "According to the map, there's an island above the clouds. An ancient place that few have ever reached. It's said to hold unimaginable secrets and... treasures."

"Treasure, you say?" Zeno raised an eyebrow, gripping his sword's hilt. "Sounds like my kind of place. What do you think, Franky?"

Franky, tinkering with the ship's sails, turned with a wide grin. "A sky island, huh? Now that's a challenge I'm all in for! We'll need to adjust the ship's altitude boosters to break through the cloud barrier."

Theo, standing nearby, piped up. "Wait, did you say 'above the clouds'? How are we even going to get up there?"

Luna smiled, leaning against the ship's railing. "We've done crazier things, Theo. I have faith we'll figure it out."

Just as she spoke, the sky began to shift. The clouds ahead started to gather, swirling in a thick, misty wall that stretched up beyond sight. The light from the sun dimmed as they drew closer to the phenomenon.

"There it is," Ryu said softly, his eyes narrowing. "The Cloud Gate."

Theo blinked. "Wait...what's a 'Cloud Gate'?"

Kaida turned to him, explaining, "It's a massive barrier of clouds that separates the sky from the legendary island. The only way to get through is to either have a ship strong enough to breach it or know the ancient route."

Franky patted the ship's side proudly. "Don't worry, this beauty is up for the challenge. I've reinforced her hull and added a few modifications. We'll shoot straight through!"

Zeno cracked his knuckles, excitement building in his eyes. "Well, no use standing around! Let's go find this island already."

With Franky adjusting the ship's boosters, the crew braced themselves as they approached the swirling clouds. The winds picked up, whipping through the sails as the ship began to climb, propelled by Franky's engineering genius. The cloud barrier loomed closer, a massive wall of mist and mystery.

"Hold on tight, everyone!" Franky shouted, gripping the controls. "This is gonna get bumpy!"

The ship shot upward, plowing through the thick cloud barrier. The mist enveloped them completely, cutting off visibility. For a moment, all they could hear was the howling of the wind and the creaking of the ship as it fought to break through.

"We're almost there!" Franky yelled over the roar.

Suddenly, the ship burst through the top of the clouds, and the mist parted, revealing a dazzling sight. Floating in the sky above them was a massive island, shimmering in the sunlight. It was a land of lush greenery, towering waterfalls cascading from floating rivers, and strange, ancient structures built from glowing stone.

Luna gasped in awe. "It's...beautiful."

Ryu, his expression serious but filled with wonder, nodded. "This must be the island of legends. We've finally made it."

Franky let out a triumphant laugh. "I told you this baby could do it! Welcome to the Skylands!"

Kaida stepped forward, scanning the landscape. "There's something off about this place. It's too quiet. If this is a legendary island, there should be people or... something."

Theo, still gripping the rail tightly from the bumpy ride, glanced around. "I don't like the looks of this. What if this place is abandoned for a reason?"

Just as he spoke, the air around them shimmered, and a low hum filled the sky. From the distant structures, figures began to emerge, gliding down from the clouds. They wore strange, ornate armor, with long, flowing capes that trailed behind them. Each one held a spear that crackled with electricity.

"They're coming right for us," Zeno said, his hand immediately going to his sword. "Looks like we've got a welcoming committee."

The leader of the group, a tall figure with an imposing presence, landed softly on the deck of their ship. His piercing eyes scanned the crew. "You trespass on sacred ground," he said, his voice deep and echoing. "Who are you, and why have you come to the Skylands?"

Ryu stepped forward, meeting the man's gaze. "We're travelers, seeking the truth about this island. We mean no harm."

The man's eyes narrowed. "No harm? This is no place for outsiders. You have disturbed the balance by coming here."

Kaida tensed, readying herself for a fight. "We didn't come here to cause trouble, but we won't back down either. If this island holds secrets, we'll uncover them."

The man smirked, his spear crackling with energy. "Then you will face the judgment of the Skyborn."

Zeno drew his sword, its edge gleaming in the sunlight. "I guess negotiations are off the table then?"

Before the man could respond, the other Skyborn soldiers charged, their spears aimed at the crew. Franky grinned, cracking his knuckles. "Looks like it's time to show them what we've got!"

Theo raised his hands, summoning a shield of energy to protect the crew from the incoming attack. "They're fast!"

Ryu's eyes glowed with determination as he unleashed his power. "Then we'll have to be faster."

The battle began in earnest as the crew clashed with the Skyborn warriors, their abilities lighting up the deck. The sound of metal against metal echoed through the skies, and the island ahead beckoned, filled with untold mysteries and dangers.

Their journey had just begun, but the challenges of the Skylands would test them like never before.

The clang of steel filled the air as the crew battled against the Skyborn soldiers. Each warrior moved with unnatural grace, their spears crackling with electricity. Ryu sidestepped an incoming thrust, eyes narrowing as he swung a fist at his opponent. His attack landed with a satisfying impact, sending the Skyborn staggering back.

"You guys aren't giving up, huh?" Ryu muttered, shifting his stance. His eyes glowed faintly as he channeled the energy within him. "Guess we're doing this the hard way!"

The leader of the Skyborn sneered, his voice cutting through the noise. "You've chosen your fate, outsiders! The Skylands will not tolerate intruders!"

Kaida parried an incoming spear with her blade, gritting her teeth as the force of the blow vibrated through her arms. "We didn't come here to fight! But if this is what it takes to survive, then we won't back down!"

The Skyborn leader laughed darkly, his spear spinning with a flourish. "Survive? You're fools if you think you can defy the laws of the Skylands."

Luna, crouched behind a barrel to catch her breath, called out to the crew, "There's too many of them! We need a plan!"

Zeno, already locked in combat with two Skyborn, glanced over his shoulder. "A plan, huh? Well, right now the only plan I've got is not to die."

Franky, fending off an enemy with his massive arms, grinned as he caught Zeno's words. "I like that plan! But how about we throw in a little smash-and-dash for good measure?"

Ryu, dodging another spear, growled, "Franky, this isn't the time for jokes!"

The Skyborn leader's eyes flashed with disdain as he glided toward Ryu, spear raised high. "Let's see how long you last against the judgment of the Skyborn!" His spear crackled with electric energy, and with a quick thrust, he lunged at Ryu.

In a flash, Ryu caught the spear with both hands, the electricity surging through his body. His muscles tensed as the power coursed through him, but he gritted his teeth and held firm. "You think this is enough to stop me?!"

With a roar, Ryu twisted the spear out of the Skyborn leader's grasp, sending him stumbling back. The crew gasped, eyes wide as Ryu's body began to glow with a faint golden light.

Luna's voice was shaky as she whispered, "Is he... unlocking his power again?"

Kaida, still holding her ground against a Skyborn warrior, nodded, her face set with determination. "Looks like it. But that power takes a toll on him... we need to finish this fast."

The Skyborn leader's eyes flickered with something akin to fear as he regained his balance, glaring at Ryu. "You... you dare use forbidden powers in the Skylands?! You'll bring down the wrath of the gods themselves!"

Ryu's grin was feral, the light around him intensifying. "Let them come! I'm done holding back!"

But just as Ryu prepared to unleash his power, Theo's voice cut through the chaos, panicked and urgent. "Ryu! Wait! If you use too much of that energy again, you'll burn yourself out!"

Ryu hesitated, his expression shifting as Theo's warning sank in. The golden glow dimmed slightly, but his resolve didn't waver. "I'll be fine. We have to end this now, or we'll never make it to the island."

Franky, still brawling with one of the soldiers, gave a quick glance toward Ryu. "Theo's right, man. You've already pushed yourself once today. We need a smarter move, not just brute force."

Zeno, locked in a fierce duel with his own opponent, shouted over his shoulder, "Leave it to me. You focus on conserving your energy. I've got this."

Ryu clenched his fists, the internal struggle clear on his face. His body was ready to unleash everything, but his mind knew the risks. "Fine," he muttered, stepping back slightly. "But don't take too long."

Zeno grinned, his blade gleaming in the sunlight. "I wouldn't dream of it."

With a swift motion, Zeno dashed toward the Skyborn leader, his sword flashing in a series of precise strikes. The leader barely had time to react, raising his spear to parry, but Zeno was too fast. His blade hummed with power, each strike sending sparks flying as it collided with the leader's weapon.

The two warriors moved at incredible speed, a blur of motion as they clashed again and again. Zeno's focus was razor-sharp, his every move calculated. "You talk big," he said between strikes, "but can you keep up?"

The Skyborn leader's expression twisted into a snarl. "You think you can defeat me, outsider?! I am one of the Skylands' elite! You will kneel before our might!"

Zeno smirked, his blade swinging in a wide arc. "Kneel? I don't kneel for anyone."

The Skyborn leader growled and unleashed a surge of electricity, but Zeno anticipated the move. With a quick twist, he avoided the attack and brought his sword down with a powerful slash. The blade crackled with energy as it met the leader's spear, sending a shockwave through the air.

Kaida, watching from the corner of her eye as she fought off another enemy, shouted, "Zeno! Don't let him control the pace of the fight! Stay on the offensive!"

"I know!" Zeno shouted back, his grin never fading. "Trust me, I've got this under control!"

But just as Zeno landed another blow, the Skyborn leader's eyes glowed with a dangerous light. "You've underestimated the power of the Skylands, boy! Witness the true might of a Skyborn warrior!"

In an instant, the leader's spear crackled with intense energy, the air around it shimmering with heat. Zeno's eyes widened as the spear thrust forward with blinding speed, aimed straight for his heart.

Time seemed to slow as Zeno's instincts kicked in. He twisted his body, narrowly avoiding the deadly thrust, but the tip of the spear grazed his side, sending a jolt of electricity through him.

"Zeno!" Luna cried out, fear gripping her heart as she watched her crewmate stagger from the blow.

Zeno gritted his teeth, fighting through the pain. "I'm... fine," he muttered, raising his sword again. "This isn't over."

The Skyborn leader smirked, his spear still crackling with energy. "Oh, it will be. Soon."

As the battle raged on, the crew knew that this was only the beginning. The island beyond the clouds held more than just treasure and secrets—it held the key to their survival. And they weren't leaving until they unlocked its mysteries.

But first, they had to win this fight.

Zeno's breath came in heavy gasps as he wiped the sweat from his brow. His side still stung where the Skyborn leader's spear had grazed him. The electricity from the attack was still coursing through his veins, making his movements sluggish.

The Skyborn leader stood tall, his eyes gleaming with the arrogance of a man who believed victory was inevitable. "You can't win," he sneered. "You're outmatched, outclassed, and clearly out of your depth."

Zeno raised his sword, smirking despite the pain. "Is that right? I've heard that before, but it never really stuck."

The leader's grip tightened on his spear. "You're just a fool, flailing with a blade you can barely control. You don't stand a chance against the true power of the Skyborn!"

Zeno's smirk widened as his mind raced. His sword felt different in his hand, as if it was resonating with something deep inside him.

He could feel a strange connection to the blade, a warmth that spread through his arm. It wasn't just a weapon anymore — it was an extension of himself.

"Control, huh?" Zeno muttered to himself. He glanced down at the sword, his eyes narrowing in focus. "Maybe it's time I show you what real control looks like."

The Skyborn leader raised an eyebrow. "What are you mumbling about, boy?"

Zeno straightened up, his sword gleaming in the sunlight. "You're right about one thing: I haven't been using this sword to its full potential. But that's about to change."

The Skyborn leader's smirk faded as he felt a shift in the air around them. The wind seemed to swirl around Zeno, his sword glowing faintly with a strange, ethereal light. "What... what are you doing?"

Zeno's voice was calm, almost too calm. "I've been relying on brute strength for too long. But a sword... a sword is more than just metal and sharp edges. It's a tool of precision, of finesse. And now... I can control every inch of it."

With a swift motion, Zeno swung his sword, but the blade never touched the Skyborn leader. In fact, it didn't even come close. But as the blade moved, the leader flinched, his body instinctively reacting as if he had been struck.

He staggered backward, his hand flying to his chest in shock. "What... what did you do?!" He looked down, expecting to see a gaping wound, but there was nothing. His armor was intact, his skin unbroken.

Zeno's grin widened. "What's wrong? You seem... startled."

The Skyborn leader's eyes darted around, panic creeping into his voice. "You didn't even hit me!"

Zeno slowly twirled the sword in his hand, the glow intensifying. "Didn't I? Or are you just too slow to realize it?"

The leader's heart pounded in his chest. He looked down again, his hand trembling as it moved over his body, searching for the wound that wasn't there. But the fear wouldn't leave. His mind told him he had been cut, that the blade had sliced through him. The pain was real, even though the injury was not.

"I... I..." The leader's voice wavered, his grip on his spear loosening.

Zeno took a step forward, his eyes locked onto the leader's. "You feel it, don't you? That fear creeping up your spine. You're starting to doubt yourself. Did I cut you or not? That's the question, right?"

The Skyborn leader stumbled back, his composure unraveling. "It's... it's a trick! You're trying to mess with my head!"

Zeno's sword shimmered as he raised it again. "Maybe. But the question is... can you afford to take that chance?"

With another swift slash, Zeno swung his blade, and once again, the leader flinched, his body reacting as if he'd been hit. This time, he cried out in pain, clutching his arm as if a deep gash had opened — but there was nothing.

The Skyborn leader's mind raced. His breathing grew rapid, his confidence shattered. "I... I don't understand..."

Zeno's voice was cold, his eyes sharp. "That's the thing about swordsmanship. It's not just about hitting your target. It's about controlling the battle, controlling the mind. With this new power, I can make you believe you've been cut, even when you haven't."

Luna, still hiding behind the ship's mast, watched in awe. "What's he doing? It's like... it's like he's not even touching him, but that guy's falling apart."

Kaida, fighting off another Skyborn nearby, spared a glance toward Zeno. "It's sword manipulation. Zeno's always had incredible instincts with a blade, but this... this is something else. He's messing with that guy's perception, making him believe he's been hit when he hasn't."

Theo, shielding himself from an incoming spear attack, shouted over, "Is that even possible? To make someone feel pain that isn't real?"

Kaida nodded grimly. "In the hands of a true swordsman... yes."

The Skyborn leader's confidence had crumbled. He stumbled back, his spear now shaking in his hands. "Get away from me!" he yelled, fear overtaking his voice. "This is sorcery!"

Zeno tilted his head, his expression unreadable. "Sorcery? No. This is just a swordsman finally using his full potential."

He advanced on the leader, his sword gleaming with each step. "You've made the mistake of underestimating me from the start. And now, you're afraid. You're so convinced that I've cut you that your own mind is betraying you."

The leader's breath came in short, panicked gasps. "Stay back!" He swung his spear wildly, but his movements were erratic, unfocused.

Zeno easily dodged the attacks, his eyes never leaving the leader's. "You can keep fighting, but it won't change anything. The moment I took control of this fight, you were already finished."

The Skyborn leader screamed in frustration, thrusting his spear forward in a final, desperate attack. But Zeno was faster. With one fluid motion, he dodged the spear and brought his sword down in a sweeping arc.

The blade stopped inches from the leader's neck.

The leader froze, his body trembling. He could feel the cold steel, even though it hadn't touched him. His entire body screamed in fear, convinced that he was moments from death.

Zeno's voice was calm, almost mocking. "And just like that... you lose."

For a long moment, the Skyborn leader stood paralyzed, his eyes wide in terror. Then, with a defeated sigh, he collapsed to his knees, his spear falling from his hands.

Zeno stepped back, sheathing his sword with a satisfied smirk. "I didn't even need to cut you."

The crew stared in disbelief, the battle around them momentarily forgotten. Luna was the first to break the silence. "Zeno... that was... incredible."

Zeno shrugged, though a small smile tugged at the corners of his lips. "Just doing my part."

Kaida grinned, a look of pride in her eyes. "Looks like you've unlocked something special there, Zeno."

He nodded, his hand resting on the hilt of his sword. "Yeah. And something tells me... we're going to need it for whatever's coming next."

The Skyborn leader lay defeated on the ground, trembling as Zeno stepped back, sheathing his sword. The eerie silence that followed the battle was soon filled with the sounds of the crew regrouping, but tension still lingered in the air. The island's strange glow pulsated from the horizon, casting long shadows as if the island itself was alive and watching them.

Zeno turned to face Kaida, Luna, and Theo, the rest of their crew now surrounding him, all staring at the downed Skyborn leader. Kaida was the first to speak.

"Zeno, that was... unlike anything I've ever seen before." Her eyes gleamed with admiration and surprise. "Sword manipulation, huh? I've heard of techniques like that, but never seen anyone actually pull it off in real combat."

Zeno shrugged, though a small, proud smile flickered across his face. "It just sort of happened. I wasn't sure if it would work, to be honest."

Luna stepped forward, her voice filled with awe. "But it wasn't just the technique. You made him believe he'd been cut... without even touching him. It's like you were inside his head."

Zeno looked at the sword in his hand, the weight of the blade feeling different now, as if it held some deeper power he was only beginning to understand. "It's not just about the blade anymore. I think... I've learned to control the very essence of it. Not just the metal, but the intent. And in battle, that intent can be more powerful than the strike itself."

Theo chuckled, wiping some sweat from his brow. "Man, I'm glad you're on our side. If you'd pulled that on me, I'd probably be running for the hills."

Zeno smirked, sliding his sword back into its sheath. "Lucky for you, I'm not in the habit of terrorizing my own crew."

Kaida's smile faded as her gaze shifted toward the horizon, where the strange glow was coming from. "But this... Sky Island or whatever it is... there's something more going on here. That leader was willing to die to stop us from reaching it."

Luna nodded, a thoughtful expression on her face. "We need to be prepared. We've been through a lot, but this place feels different. It's not like any of the islands we've visited before. Something tells me we're stepping into a whole new kind of danger."

Zeno crossed his arms, his eyes narrowing. "Whatever it is, we'll handle it. We've come this far, haven't we?"

Theo looked back toward the docks where the remnants of the Skyborn army were retreating, licking their wounds from the battle. "Those guys won't be our only problem. There are probably more enemies waiting for us the deeper we go."

Kaida placed a hand on her sword, her expression serious. "And we'll face them together. But for now, we need to regroup and figure out what's ahead. If this island holds some kind of power or secret, we need to find it before anyone else does."

Before anyone could respond, a loud rustling came from the treeline. The crew instantly snapped into defensive stances, their weapons drawn. From the shadows emerged a figure—large, hulking, and familiar.

"Franky?" Theo's voice broke the tension as he recognized their ally.

Franky grinned, his large frame covered in dirt and scratches from his recent battle. "Looks like you guys handled the party without me," he said, his voice booming. "I ran into a few... complications."

Kaida laughed, the tension in her shoulders easing slightly. "Good to see you in one piece, Franky. We were starting to worry."

Franky flexed his massive arms, cracking his knuckles with a smirk. "It's gonna take a lot more than a couple of Skyborn lackeys to take me down. But we've got bigger problems."

Zeno raised an eyebrow. "What kind of problems?"

Franky's expression turned serious as he gestured toward the strange glow on the horizon. "That island you're heading toward... it's not just some ordinary land. The Skyborn call it the 'Island of Ascension.' It's a place where only the strongest can survive, and it's said to hold power beyond our imagination. But there's a catch. Not everyone who goes there comes back."

Luna frowned, glancing at the glow in the distance. "Why does every island we visit come with some sort of terrifying legend?"

Franky crossed his arms, his voice low. "This isn't just a legend. I've seen what that place can do. It draws in those who seek power, but not all of them leave... at least not the same as when they arrived."

Zeno's hand unconsciously tightened around his sword hilt. "So, it's a place that either makes you stronger... or breaks you."

Kaida stepped forward, her gaze never leaving the glowing horizon. "We don't have a choice. If there's something dangerous on that island, we need to find it before it finds us. And if this 'power' is real, we'll have to make sure it doesn't fall into the wrong hands."

Franky looked hesitant for the first time since they'd met him. "I know you're all strong, but this island... it's not like anything we've faced before. There's a reason they call it the Island of Ascension. It changes people. Are you sure you're ready for that?"

Zeno glanced at his crewmates, determination burning in his eyes. "We've been through hell and back already, Franky. Whatever this island throws at us, we'll face it head-on."

Theo nodded in agreement, his usual laid-back demeanor replaced with a serious edge. "We didn't come this far to turn back now."

Kaida gave a firm nod, her eyes blazing with resolve. "We're ready."

Franky let out a deep sigh, though a small smile crept onto his face. "You're a stubborn bunch, I'll give you that. Alright, I'll come with you to the Island of Ascension. If anyone's gonna survive that place, it's you lot."

Luna smiled, though a hint of worry lingered in her expression. "Thanks, Franky. We'll need all the help we can get."

As the crew gathered their strength and prepared to set sail, Kaida turned to Zeno, her expression softening. "That power you used earlier... the sword manipulation... can you control it now?"

Zeno looked down at his sword, the blade reflecting the dying light of the day. "I don't know," he admitted quietly. "It feels like the sword is an extension of me now, like it's alive. But controlling it... that's still new to me."

Kaida placed a reassuring hand on his shoulder. "Whatever it is, we'll figure it out together. Just don't lose yourself in it."

Zeno nodded, grateful for her support. "I won't."

The crew boarded their ship, the wind carrying them toward the glowing island on the horizon. The Island of Ascension awaited them, and with it, new challenges, new enemies, and a power that could change their fates forever.

As they sailed forward, Theo leaned over the side of the ship, his eyes scanning the waters. "Hey, Franky, you're sure there's nothing lurking in these waters, right?"

Franky laughed, the sound booming across the deck. "Relax, kid. Nothing's gonna pop out and bite you... probably."

Luna chuckled, nudging Theo playfully. "I think that's Franky's way of saying we're on our own from here."

Kaida stood at the helm, her gaze locked on the glowing horizon. "Whatever happens next, we face it together. No matter what this island throws at us... we'll overcome it."

Zeno stood beside her, his hand resting on the hilt of his sword, ready for whatever lay ahead. "Yeah... together."

The wind swept through the sails of their ship, carrying the crew toward the glowing island ahead. The eerie light from the Island of Ascension flickered like a beacon, both inviting and foreboding. The crew had been sailing for hours, their conversations turning to quiet murmurs as they prepared for whatever challenges awaited them.

Ryu stood near the bow of the ship, his arms crossed as he stared intently at the horizon. His sharp eyes scanned the waters, narrowing in focus. Something wasn't right. The way the waves moved, the faint shimmer in the distance—it was as if the sea itself was trying to conceal something.

He turned to face the rest of the crew, his voice breaking the silence. "I see something up ahead," Ryu said, his tone calm but laced with caution.

Zeno, who had been leaning against the mast, looked up from his thoughts. "What is it? Another ship?"

Ryu shook his head, still squinting toward the horizon. "No... it's not a ship. It's something in the water. But I can't tell what. The surface... it's moving differently, like there's something beneath it."

Kaida, standing by the helm, glanced over at him with concern. "Something beneath the water? Could it be a sea creature?"

Franky, who had been polishing one of his mechanical arms, straightened up at Ryu's words. "Sea creatures this close to the island? That doesn't sound good. The legends about this place mention all kinds of weird things happening, but I didn't think it'd start before we even reached the shore."

Theo, sitting on a barrel nearby, stood up, trying to get a better view. "You sure it's not just the light from the island messing with the water? The glow from that place could be making things look strange."

Ryu shook his head, his eyes still fixed on the horizon. "No, this is different. The water's moving too erratically. It's like there's something... shifting underneath it."

Luna, her brow furrowed, walked over to Ryu's side, peering out into the distance. "Could it be a trap? If this island's as dangerous as everyone says, there could be something waiting for us before we even make landfall."

Ryu's jaw tightened, his gaze never wavering. "It's possible. But we're not turning back now. We just need to be ready for whatever it is."

Zeno, always eager for a challenge, stepped forward, hand resting casually on the hilt of his sword. "If something's trying to stop us, let it try. We've handled worse."

Kaida, though usually the voice of reason, couldn't help but feel a sense of unease creeping over her. "We shouldn't underestimate this place. Everything about it feels... off. We need to be on guard."

Franky nodded in agreement. "She's right. I've seen places like this before—places where the rules of the world don't apply like they should. This island feels like one of them. If something's in the water, it might not just be a sea creature. It could be... something else entirely."

Theo groaned, his usual lightheartedness fading. "Why can't we ever land on a nice, normal island? You know, with beaches and coconuts? Maybe a friendly village? We're always heading straight into some nightmare scenario."

Luna gave him a playful nudge. "Wouldn't be much of an adventure if it was easy, would it?"

Theo sighed dramatically. "I was fine with adventure until it involved sea monsters and glowing islands."

Ryu cut through the banter, his tone more urgent now. "Everyone, get ready. Whatever this is, it's coming closer."

The crew quickly snapped to attention, the relaxed atmosphere dissolving into focused readiness. Zeno unsheathed his sword, the blade gleaming in the faint light, while Kaida tightened her grip on the helm, steering them toward what awaited. Luna moved to the ship's edge, her eyes scanning the water for any movement, while Theo muttered to himself, checking his weapons nervously.

And then, as if responding to Ryu's heightened senses, the water ahead began to churn violently. Massive bubbles rose to the surface, creating ripples that spread outward, making the ship rock gently with each wave.

"There! You see that?" Ryu pointed toward the epicenter of the disturbance. "Something's coming up."

Franky's eyes widened as he leaned over the railing. "That's no ordinary sea creature. Look at the size of those bubbles. Whatever's down there is massive."

Suddenly, the ship lurched as something huge brushed against its underside, the impact sending a shockwave through the deck. The crew staggered, grabbing onto the nearest stable surface to avoid being thrown off balance.

"What the hell was that?!" Theo shouted, his eyes wide with panic.

Before anyone could answer, the water erupted with a deafening roar. A gigantic shape broke through the surface, casting a towering shadow over the ship. It was an enormous serpent-like creature, its scales glistening in the strange glow of the island, eyes glowing with an unnatural, malevolent light.

Zeno grinned, a spark of excitement flashing in his eyes. "Now *that's* more like it."

Kaida, still gripping the helm, called out to the crew. "Brace yourselves! This thing's not going to let us pass easily!"

Ryu stood tall at the bow, his eyes locked onto the serpent as it circled the ship. "This isn't just a sea creature. It's something else—something tied to the island's power."

Luna gripped her weapon tightly, her stance ready for battle. "Do we fight it? Or try to outrun it?"

Franky cracked his knuckles, a determined grin spreading across his face. "Looks like we don't have much of a choice. If we don't take this thing down, we're not getting anywhere near that island."

Theo, still gripping his weapons, gulped audibly. "I knew it! I knew something was going to jump out of the water! Why does it always have to be giant sea monsters?!"

Ryu's voice cut through the chaos, calm but commanding. "Theo, focus. We're going to need your explosives if we're going to take this thing down."

Theo nodded quickly, shaking off his nerves. "Right! Explosives. Got it!"

Zeno stepped forward, his sword drawn, eyes gleaming with anticipation. "Let's make this quick. The longer we're out here, the more time we're wasting."

Kaida, her face set in determination, gave the final order. "Everyone, prepare for battle! We take this thing down, and we keep moving forward!"

As the serpent circled again, preparing for its next strike, the crew readied themselves. The air crackled with tension, the island's strange light casting everything in an ominous glow. The battle for the Island of Ascension was about to begin.

The tension in the air was palpable as the massive serpent loomed above the crew, its glowing eyes locking onto them with a predatory gaze. The creature's coils slithered beneath the water, creating massive waves that rocked the ship back and forth.

Ryu stood at the bow, his fists clenched, muscles taut as he prepared himself. "Everyone, stay sharp! We don't know how this thing fights, but we're not backing down."

Zeno gripped his sword tighter, eyes locked on the serpent as it hissed, revealing rows of jagged teeth. "It's been a while since we've fought something this big," he muttered, a grin creeping onto his face. "I've missed this kind of fight."

Theo, crouched behind the mast, peeked around cautiously. "I didn't miss it," he mumbled under his breath. "Big sea monsters aren't exactly my idea of fun."

Luna, standing beside him, gave him a sideways glance. "You always say that, but when the fight starts, you're usually the first one to jump in."

Theo looked flustered. "That's because I'm trying to survive! I'm not doing it because I enjoy it!"

Ryu's eyes flicked over to Theo. "You'll enjoy surviving this fight if you focus. Theo, get the explosives ready. We'll need them if this thing tries to wrap around the ship."

Theo's eyes widened, realizing what Ryu meant. "Explosives? Around the ship? Oh, great. No pressure," he grumbled, fumbling to grab the small packs of dynamite he kept for emergencies.

Kaida kept her hands steady on the helm, steering them slightly away from the serpent's direct path, but the creature was too fast. It reared up out of the water, its enormous head towering over the ship.

"Incoming!" Kaida shouted, her voice cutting through the roar of the waves.

With a deafening hiss, the serpent lunged toward the deck, its maw wide open, aiming to devour them whole. Zeno was the first to act. With a flash of steel, he dashed forward, his sword glowing faintly as he swung it in a wide arc.

"Let's see how tough you really are!" Zeno shouted, his blade making contact with the serpent's scales.

There was a sharp clang as his sword struck the creature's hide, but the blow barely scratched it. Zeno's eyes narrowed as he leapt back, avoiding the serpent's snapping jaws. "Its scales are tougher than I thought," he muttered.

Ryu nodded. "That's why we hit it where it's weakest."

The serpent lashed out again, its tail whipping across the water, sending another wave crashing into the ship. Luna struggled to maintain her balance, gripping the railing as the ship tilted.

Theo stumbled beside her, barely managing to hold onto the dynamite. "This is insane! We're fighting a sea monster with dynamite! Does anyone else see the problem here?"

Luna smirked. "Relax. We've done crazier things."

Franky, who had been quiet until now, stepped forward, his mechanical arm clicking as it transformed into a massive cannon. "Less talking, more fighting," he said, his deep voice steady as ever.

The serpent reared back again, and Franky aimed his arm toward its head. "Let's see how you like this, big guy!" He fired a powerful blast from his arm cannon, the explosion sending a ball of energy toward the serpent.

The blast struck the creature's jaw, forcing it to pull back with a screech. The attack stunned it for a moment, but it wasn't enough to stop it.

Ryu's eyes darted toward Zeno. "Zeno, aim for its eyes. They're vulnerable."

Zeno nodded, already moving. "On it!"

As the serpent shook off Franky's blast and lunged again, Zeno dashed across the deck, leaping into the air. His sword glowed brighter as he summoned his newfound ability. "Sword Manipulation!" Zeno called out, his voice filled with determination.

In mid-air, Zeno swung his sword downward toward the serpent's eye. But as the blade came close, it seemed to vanish for a split second—then reappeared, cutting a path directly through the serpent's gaze.

The creature let out a horrendous screech, recoiling in pain. But as Zeno landed, the crew realized something strange had happened. The serpent's eye wasn't damaged at all. It had been an illusion, a trick Zeno's sword had played on both the serpent and the crew.

Luna's eyes widened. "Did he just—?"

"He didn't cut it... but it *thinks* he did," Theo finished, shaking his head in disbelief.

Zeno smirked, looking down at his sword. "This power... it's trickier than I thought, but it works."

The serpent, confused and now enraged, lashed out wildly, its massive tail crashing down onto the deck. The crew scattered, narrowly avoiding the impact.

Ryu, dodging the attack, landed near the center of the ship. His gaze remained focused on the serpent. "Franky, hit it again! We need to keep it off balance!"

Franky nodded, charging his arm cannon for another shot. "Don't worry, I've got plenty more where that came from!"

Theo, still clutching the explosives, looked to Ryu. "When do I throw these?!"

Ryu's eyes narrowed. "When its head goes under the ship. We can't let it drag us down."

The serpent, still recovering from Zeno's trick, circled back around, preparing to strike again. This time, it dove beneath the water, disappearing for a moment before surfacing on the other side of the ship.

Kaida's eyes widened. "It's going for the hull!"

"Now, Theo!" Ryu shouted.

With shaking hands, Theo lit the fuse and hurled the explosives over the side of the ship. They hit the water just as the serpent surged upward, and with a thunderous explosion, the sea erupted in a massive plume of water and smoke.

The serpent screamed in agony, its body thrashing as the explosion rocked it from below. But despite the damage, it wasn't finished.

Zeno, seeing the opportunity, dashed forward again, his sword glowing with energy. "Let's finish this!"

He leapt into the air, swinging his sword in another arc. This time, the serpent's body convulsed as if struck by an invisible force, and the creature's movements slowed.

Ryu nodded in approval, his voice calm amidst the chaos. "Good. Now we have the advantage."

But as the serpent writhed in pain, something caught Ryu's eye. Just beyond the creature, on the island's shore, a massive structure began to emerge from the mist—a tower, glowing with the same strange light as the island itself.

"Everyone, look!" Ryu shouted, pointing toward the island. "There's something on the shore... a tower. That's where we're heading."

Kaida's gaze followed Ryu's finger, her eyes narrowing. "So that's our destination. But we have to get past this thing first."

Franky, his arm cannon still smoking, grinned. "Then let's finish it off and make our way there."

The crew readied themselves for the final strike, their eyes locked on the wounded serpent. The battle was far from over, but the path ahead was becoming clearer.

The serpent reared back, its body thrashing wildly, causing the ship to sway dangerously. The waves grew larger, crashing against the hull as the sea itself seemed to react to the creature's fury.

Ryu wiped the sweat from his brow and glanced at the crew. "Hold steady! We're not done yet."

Suddenly, without warning, the serpent opened its massive jaws, glowing orbs of energy beginning to form in its mouth. The crew's eyes widened in horror.

"Is it charging up an attack?!" Theo shouted, backing away from the edge of the ship.

Luna's voice was sharp, cutting through the rising panic. "Everyone, brace yourselves!"

Franky, still readying his cannon arm, looked over his shoulder. "That thing's gonna blast us to pieces if we don't stop it!"

Before anyone could react, the serpent unleashed a barrage of glowing energy bombs, each one hurtling through the air like falling stars. The sky lit up with flashes of light, and the crew scattered to avoid the incoming destruction.

The first explosion hit the deck, shaking the entire ship with the force of the impact. Wood splintered, and flames erupted, sending debris flying in all directions.

"Get down!" Zeno yelled, diving behind a stack of barrels as another explosion tore through the air.

Kaida gripped the helm with all her strength, trying to steer the ship out of the serpent's range. "It's no use! We're right in its line of fire!"

A third blast hit the side of the ship, sending a massive wave of water over the deck. The crew was soaked, struggling to keep their footing as the ship was tossed about like a toy.

Ryu narrowed his eyes, sensing something terrible coming. He could feel the serpent's energy building, a final, devastating strike.

"We can't let it destroy the ship," he said, his voice low but determined. Without a moment's hesitation, Ryu ran toward the edge of the deck.

Zeno caught a glimpse of Ryu's movement and called out, "Ryu! What are you doing?!"

"I'm going to stop it before it's too late!" Ryu shouted back, leaping over the railing and into the crashing waves below.

"Ryu, no!" Luna screamed, rushing to the side of the ship, but it was too late. Ryu had already disappeared into the stormy waters.

The crew watched in shock as the sea swallowed their captain. Zeno clenched his fists, his knuckles turning white as the rain began to fall harder. "What was he thinking?"

Luna turned to him, panic in her voice. "We need to get him back! He's going to drown!"

Theo's eyes darted between the waves and the serpent, which was still charging another attack. "We can't go after him! Not while this thing's still attacking!"

Luna shook her head frantically, refusing to accept it. "We can't just leave him out there! He won't make it!"

Zeno's gaze hardened. "We don't have a choice. Ryu knew what he was doing. He trusted us to finish the fight." He turned to the others, his voice steady but strained. "Focus on the battle. We'll get Ryu back when this is over."

Kaida shouted from the helm, "This thing's not giving up. If we don't end it now, none of us will survive long enough to save anyone!"

Franky grunted, adjusting his cannon arm. "Then let's end this!" He aimed at the serpent again, firing another blast toward its head. "This one's for you, Ryu!"

The explosion hit the serpent's side, causing it to reel back with a furious scream. But the beast was relentless, diving beneath the waves for another assault.

Meanwhile, beneath the surface, Ryu struggled against the powerful currents. The cold water pressed in around him as he sank deeper into the dark abyss. He could feel his strength fading, the weight of the sea pulling him down.

He gasped for air, but only seawater filled his lungs. His vision blurred as he looked up toward the surface, the light of the ship dimming. His limbs felt heavy, and for the first time, a chilling thought crept into his mind.

Is this it? Is this where it ends?

But even as his body gave in to the water's grasp, something deep within him stirred—a burning energy that refused to be extinguished. His eyes flickered with determination, and in the darkness, he clenched his fists.

I can't go down like this. Not yet. Not when they need me.

Back on the ship, Luna was still standing at the railing, her knuckles white as she gripped the wood. She could barely hear anything over the roar of the storm and the serpent's relentless assault.

"Zeno!" she yelled over the noise. "What if he's already—"

"Don't say it!" Zeno snapped, his eyes locked on the serpent as he parried one of its massive strikes with his sword. "Ryu's not dead. Not yet. We'll save him when this is over!"

Theo scrambled to light more explosives, tossing them toward the serpent in a desperate attempt to keep it at bay. "Can't believe we're doing this while our captain's drowning!"

The ship creaked under the pressure of another explosion, and Kaida struggled to keep them afloat. "We won't survive much longer if we don't end this soon!"

The serpent reappeared, its glowing eyes fixed on the ship as it prepared another energy bomb.

Zeno tightened his grip on his sword, his brow furrowed in concentration. "This ends now. We're getting Ryu back."

As the serpent loomed closer, ready to unleash its final attack, the crew readied themselves for the onslaught. They had no choice but to fight, their hearts heavy with the knowledge that their captain was sinking deeper into the sea with every passing moment.

But even in the darkness, Ryu wasn't done fighting.

As the serpent prepared to unleash another devastating attack on the crew, the sea churned violently beneath them. Thunder rumbled across the sky, and lightning flashed ominously, illuminating the chaos around the ship. But then, something strange happened—a massive whirlpool began to form near where Ryu had plunged into the sea.

The crew felt the ship lurch, struggling to keep balance as the whirlpool grew larger by the second.

"What's going on now?!" Theo yelled, clutching a railing as the wind picked up.

"It's the sea! Something's happening!" Luna shouted, eyes wide with panic. She glanced over the edge, her voice trembling. "Is that where Ryu went under?"

Zeno's grip tightened on his sword, the storm making it harder to focus on both the serpent and whatever was happening below. "What in the world is that? Some kind of sea beast?"

The serpent, seemingly unnerved by the sudden shift in the waters, reared back, its glowing eyes watching the whirlpool suspiciously. For the first time, it hesitated, unsure of its next move.

Kaida, steering the ship with all her might, shouted over the roar of the ocean. "Everyone, hang on! The sea's trying to drag us in!"

Franky squinted toward the center of the whirlpool, watching as the water swirled faster and faster. "Wait... is that...?"

Just then, the whirlpool exploded upward in a massive burst of water, creating a towering wave that crashed against the side of the ship. The force of it nearly knocked everyone off their feet, but in the chaos, a figure shot up from the depths of the sea.

"RYU!" Luna screamed, her voice filled with both relief and disbelief.

With a powerful leap, Ryu soared through the air, his body glowing faintly with the remnants of the energy he had unlocked beneath the waves. Water dripped from his clothes and hair, but his eyes were sharp and focused, filled with a renewed determination. As he neared the ship, he twisted midair, using the wind to propel himself toward the deck.

Theo watched in awe, his jaw dropping. "He's alive?!"

Ryu landed gracefully on the ship's deck with a heavy thud, crouching for a brief moment before standing tall. His chest rose and fell with heavy breaths, but there was a fire in his eyes that hadn't been there before. He glanced at the serpent, then back at his crew.

Zeno was the first to step forward, his usual stoic expression cracking into one of relief. "Ryu... you crazy bastard."

Ryu smirked, his voice hoarse but steady. "Took a little swim. Had to cool off."

Luna practically ran to him, stopping just short of grabbing him. Her face was a mixture of anger and concern. "You idiot! You could've died! What were you thinking?!"

Ryu shrugged, wiping some water from his brow. "I had to take care of things down there. But I'm back now. And we're finishing this."

Franky, still clutching his cannon arm, let out a booming laugh. "You sure know how to make an entrance, Captain!"

Kaida grinned from the helm, her grip on the wheel still firm. "Nice to have you back. But in case you haven't noticed, we've still got a massive sea monster trying to blast us into oblivion!"

Ryu turned toward the serpent, his expression hardening. "I noticed. It's time to send this thing back to the depths."

The serpent let out a furious screech, clearly agitated by Ryu's sudden return. Its glowing eyes locked onto him, and the energy bombs in its mouth began to charge once again.

Zeno stepped forward, his sword at the ready. "We'll handle this together. You don't have to take it on alone."

Ryu shook his head, a determined look crossing his face. "No. I've got this." He looked back at his crew, giving them a confident nod. "Trust me."

Theo blinked in disbelief. "You're serious? You want to take that thing on by yourself?"

Ryu's body crackled with energy, remnants of the mysterious power still coursing through him. "I won't be alone. I've got all of you with me." He shot them a small smile. "But leave this to me. I'll end this now."

Before anyone could argue, Ryu shot forward, faster than the eye could follow. The air around him crackled with energy as he leaped toward the serpent, his fists glowing with an otherworldly light. The serpent roared in defiance, launching its energy bombs directly at him.

But Ryu didn't flinch.

With a swift motion, he dodged the incoming blasts, weaving through the serpent's attacks with incredible agility. The crew watched in awe, barely able to keep up with his movements.

"Look at him go..." Luna whispered, her eyes wide.

Zeno couldn't help but grin. "He's stronger than ever."

Ryu reached the serpent's head in an instant, his glowing fist pulled back, ready to strike. With a mighty roar, he slammed his fist into the serpent's skull, the impact sending shockwaves through the air. The force was so immense that the serpent was launched backward, crashing into the ocean with a deafening splash.

For a moment, everything was still. The serpent lay motionless in the water, its body barely visible beneath the churning waves.

Ryu landed back on the ship, breathing heavily but standing tall. He turned to his crew, a triumphant look in his eyes. "It's done."

The crew erupted into cheers, their relief palpable.

Theo ran up to Ryu, clapping him on the back. "That was incredible, Captain! You really took it down!"

Franky grinned, his mechanical hand giving Ryu a hearty pat on the back. "I knew you had it in you! The serpent didn't stand a chance!"

But Luna's expression remained serious as she approached Ryu. "Are you okay?" she asked softly, her concern evident.

Ryu nodded, though there was a flicker of exhaustion in his eyes. "I'm fine... for now."

Zeno walked over, folding his arms. "You've got some explaining to do later, you know that, right?"

Ryu smirked. "I'll fill you in. But first, let's get out of here."

The storm had begun to calm, the serpent defeated, and the crew began to steer the ship toward the horizon once more. But as they sailed away, Ryu couldn't help but glance back at the sea, his mind racing with thoughts of the strange power that had saved him.

Something told him this was only the beginning.

As the crew sailed away from the stormy waters, the calm after the battle left them feeling a mix of relief and uncertainty. The ship cut through the sea, the sun now peeking out from behind the clouds, casting a warm glow over the deck.

Zeno stood at the railing, his arms crossed and his sword sheathed at his side. He glanced back at Ryu, who was leaning against the mast, still looking slightly exhausted from the fight. Zeno's eyes narrowed in thought.

"You know you're not getting away with just a 'let's get out of here,' right?" Zeno said, his voice low but with a hint of humor.

Ryu raised an eyebrow, pushing himself off the mast with a slight smirk. "You're still on about that?"

Zeno walked over, folding his arms. "You pull off some kind of superhuman power, jump back onto the ship like nothing happened, and now we're supposed to sail into the sunset? Yeah, I'm still on about that."

Luna, overhearing their conversation, came up beside them. "He's right, Ryu. What happened back there? You went under the water and came back with... that."

Ryu rubbed the back of his neck, looking off toward the horizon. "I don't know. It just... happened."

Theo, who had been quietly listening while inspecting the ship's damage, chimed in. "You mean to tell us you don't know what that was? You were glowing, Captain. Glowing."

Ryu let out a small laugh, though it was clear he didn't have all the answers. "Yeah, I felt it. It was like this surge of power I didn't even know I had. Something in the sea... it unlocked something in me."

Kaida, still at the helm, gave them a sideways glance. "You can't just leave it at that. You unlocked some new strength, and we're not supposed to ask questions?"

Ryu's expression softened, and he sighed, sitting down on one of the barrels. "Look, I'll be honest—I don't know how it happened.

When I was underwater, I felt like I was drowning, like the sea was pulling me down. But then something clicked. I don't know if it was desperation or instinct, but I felt a shift in my body. The power—it was like it was always there, but something needed to wake it up."

Luna knelt down beside him, her voice gentle but serious. "And what happens if you use it again? Do you even know if it's safe?"

Ryu stared at his hands, clenching them into fists as if trying to feel the energy again. "I'm not sure. But we'll have to figure that out."

Zeno shook his head, a faint grin appearing on his face. "You always get us into the wildest situations, you know that? First, serpents, now mysterious sea powers. What's next, a floating island?"

Theo let out a chuckle. "At this rate, nothing would surprise me."

Franky, who had been working on some minor repairs, finally joined the conversation. "Speaking of next, what's the plan, Captain? We can't keep running into these things without a proper destination in mind."

Ryu's eyes shifted toward the open sea. "We need to reach the next island. I've got a feeling something's waiting for us there."

Kaida raised an eyebrow. "You're talking about that island you mentioned earlier—the one you saw before the serpent attack?"

Ryu nodded. "Yeah, something's off about it. I couldn't make out much, but there was a strange light coming from the center of it. It didn't look natural."

Luna's eyes widened slightly. "A light? Could it be some kind of beacon?"

"Or a trap," Zeno added, his hand resting on the hilt of his sword.

Theo shrugged. "Either way, sounds like we don't have much choice. We need supplies, and it's the closest land."

Ryu stood up, his resolve hardening. "Exactly. We're heading there. But everyone, stay alert. If something's waiting for us on that island, we're going to be ready."

Franky wiped his hands, his mechanical arm whirring softly. "I'll have the ship in top shape by the time we get there. If things go sideways, at least we'll have an escape plan."

Kaida steered the ship toward the new destination, the wind picking up slightly as they adjusted course. "I hope you're wrong about the trap, Ryu," she muttered, half to herself.

Ryu glanced at Zeno and Theo, a knowing look passing between them. "It wouldn't be the first time we've walked into something dangerous."

Zeno chuckled. "Yeah, but it's never boring."

Hours passed as they sailed toward the mysterious island. The closer they got, the more ominous the atmosphere became. The sea seemed to darken, the waves growing rougher, and an unnatural fog began to surround the ship.

Theo was the first to notice it. "This fog... it came out of nowhere."

Ryu's gaze sharpened. "Everyone, stay on your guard. Something's not right."

Luna pulled her hood over her head, looking around warily. "Do you think it's connected to that light you saw?"

"Could be," Ryu replied, scanning the horizon. "But we'll know soon enough."

As the fog thickened, the silhouette of the island finally appeared on the horizon. Dark, jagged cliffs rose from the sea, and in the center, a faint glow flickered, just as Ryu had described.

"There it is," Kaida said, her voice tense. "Doesn't look too welcoming, does it?"

Zeno unsheathed his sword, the faint hum of energy vibrating through the air. "No turning back now."

Theo cracked his knuckles. "Whatever's waiting for us, we'll handle it like we always do."

Ryu stepped forward, his eyes locked on the island. "We'll handle it together."

As they drew closer, the ship's pace slowed, the waves becoming eerily calm. The air was thick with tension, and even the wind seemed to hold its breath.

Then, just as they were about to reach the shore, a deafening roar echoed from the island, shaking the very air around them.

Luna's eyes widened in horror. "What was that?!"

Ryu narrowed his gaze, his body tensing. "Something's welcoming us."

From the depths of the fog, massive serpentine figures began to emerge, their eyes glowing with malice as they slithered through the water toward the ship.

Zeno readied his sword, the blade gleaming with newfound energy. "Looks like we've got company."

Theo grinned, cracking his neck. "About time."

Ryu took a deep breath, his voice steady but filled with anticipation. "Let's show them what we're made of."

As the serpents closed in, the crew prepared for battle, their resolve unwavering. The island loomed ahead, the light flickering like a beacon of both hope and danger.

This was only the beginning of what awaited them.

As the serpents loomed closer, the tension on the ship escalated. Their dark, scaly bodies cut through the water like blades, the glowing eyes fixed menacingly on the crew. The sea felt alive, thick with malice and danger.

Zeno gripped his sword tightly, the energy coursing through it almost palpable. "These things aren't going to make it easy, are they?" He muttered, though there was a hint of excitement in his voice.

Luna, her gaze never leaving the approaching serpents, reached for her twin daggers. "Easy was never in the cards for us, was it?" she replied, glancing sideways at Zeno with a sharp grin. "Besides, I think we've faced worse."

Theo stood at the front of the ship, cracking his knuckles in anticipation. His towering frame looked almost relaxed, but his eyes burned with the desire for action. "Just point me to the biggest one. I'll make sure it regrets ever coming near our ship."

Ryu stepped forward, his expression serious, yet focused. The strange new power he had unlocked earlier still lingered within him, but he wasn't sure how much he could rely on it. "Stay sharp, everyone," he ordered, scanning the water around them. "These serpents aren't just attacking randomly. There's something—or someone—controlling them."

Kaida, at the helm, tightened her grip on the wheel. "You think they're coming from the island? Like they're guarding it?"

"More like a warning," Ryu answered, his voice grim. "Whoever or whatever is on that island doesn't want us to get there."

Franky, standing near the ship's cannon, gave a confident nod. "Well, warning or not, they picked the wrong crew to mess with."

As the serpents neared striking distance, one of them reared its massive head, its jaws opening wide, revealing rows of razor-sharp teeth. With a deafening hiss, it lunged at the ship.

"Here it comes!" Luna shouted, her daggers flashing as she prepared for the strike.

Zeno was already in motion. His sword blazed with a brilliant glow, and in a single, fluid motion, he slashed downward. The air hummed with energy, and the serpent was seemingly cleaved in two. But as Zeno's sword finished its arc, the creature was still intact, the cut only an illusion. The serpent faltered, confused, before recoiling back into the water.

Zeno smirked, sheathing his sword briefly. "Sword manipulation," he muttered under his breath. "It makes them think they've been hit... but they haven't."

Luna laughed, impressed. "That's a neat trick, Zeno. Got any more surprises up your sleeve?"

Zeno shrugged casually. "Guess you'll have to wait and see."

Another serpent lunged from the left, its body winding like a coiled spring. This time, Theo reacted, launching himself at the creature with a roar. His fist collided with the side of the serpent's jaw, sending a shockwave through the air. The serpent let out a guttural screech as it was sent flying back into the sea.

"One down," Theo said with a smirk, brushing off his hands as if it were nothing.

But more serpents were emerging from the depths, their numbers seemingly endless. Ryu's eyes narrowed as he stepped to the edge of the ship. "There's too many of them," he said quietly, his mind racing for a plan. "If we keep fighting like this, we'll get overwhelmed."

Kaida's voice called out from the helm. "We need to get to the island. It's our only chance! If we stay out here, we'll be fighting them forever."

Zeno nodded in agreement, eyeing the serpents warily. "She's right. We need to make a break for it. These things aren't going to stop unless we get out of their territory."

Ryu thought for a moment before turning to Franky. "Can you give us more speed?"

Franky gave him a sharp grin. "You bet. Just hold on tight."

He moved quickly to the engine room, adjusting gears and cranking up the ship's speed. The vessel lurched forward as the sails caught more wind, cutting through the water faster than before.

But the serpents weren't giving up. Several of them coiled their bodies around the ship's hull, slowing its momentum.

"They're trying to stop us!" Luna shouted, her daggers flashing as she struck at the serpents clinging to the ship.

Theo grabbed one by the neck, wrestling it off and tossing it into the water. "We've gotta shake them off!"

Ryu's brow furrowed. "I'll take care of it."

Without hesitation, he ran to the side of the ship and leapt into the air, his body glowing faintly again as he activated the new power that had saved him earlier. His fists crackled with energy as he descended toward one of the serpents coiling around the hull.

With a mighty punch, he sent a shockwave through the creature's body, forcing it to release its grip and slither away. "Go!" Ryu shouted as he landed back on the deck, panting heavily from the exertion.

Zeno dashed to his side, giving him a nod of respect. "Nice move, Captain. But don't burn yourself out just yet."

Ryu grinned, though his breathing was still heavy. "I'll be fine. Let's just get to that island."

The crew continued fighting off the remaining serpents, each working in sync to keep the ship moving. With every serpent that lunged at them, they retaliated fiercely, slowly but surely gaining the upper hand.

Finally, as the ship neared the shore, the serpents began to retreat, hissing as they disappeared into the depths. The crew stood on the deck, battered but victorious, as the island loomed closer.

Luna wiped sweat from her brow, her expression cautious. "We made it... but something tells me the real challenge is just beginning."

Theo stretched, cracking his knuckles again. "Good. I was just getting warmed up."

Zeno looked out at the island, his eyes narrowing. "That light Ryu saw... it's not natural. We need to stay on guard."

Ryu, still catching his breath, gave a curt nod. "We're here for answers—and I think we're going to find more than we bargained for."

As the ship docked at the mysterious island, the fog began to lift, revealing a vast, ancient city hidden within the cliffs. The strange light flickered once more from its center, almost like it was beckoning them.

Ryu stepped forward, leading the way. "Let's go."

And with that, the crew set foot on the island, unaware of the dark secrets that awaited them.

As Ryu led the crew onto the island, they stepped onto a cobblestone path that wound through dense foliage and towering trees. The air was thick with mystery, and an eerie silence hung over them, broken only by the distant rustling of leaves and the occasional call of exotic birds.

"This place feels... ancient," Kaida said, her voice barely above a whisper. She glanced around, eyes wide with wonder and unease. "Like it hasn't been touched in centuries."

Zeno, still holding his sword loosely at his side, nodded. "Yeah, and it's definitely hiding something. The atmosphere is charged. I can feel it."

Luna, staying close to Ryu, looked up at the sky, where the sun was starting to set, casting long shadows across the ground. "That light—it's coming from the center of the island, right? We should head there."

Theo cracked his knuckles again, a grin spreading across his face. "I'm ready for whatever's waiting for us. Let's get to that light!"

Ryu raised a hand to pause them. "Wait. We should be cautious. This place could be filled with traps or hidden enemies."

As they continued down the path, the trees began to thin out, revealing glimpses of ancient stone structures partially covered in vines and moss. Ryu's heart raced; there was a beauty to the decay, but it felt almost alive, as if the island itself was watching them.

"Look at that," Zeno said, pointing to a large archway ahead, adorned with intricate carvings of serpents and mythical creatures. "That has to lead to the heart of the island."

Luna stepped closer, studying the carvings. "These designs... they remind me of the serpents we fought earlier. Maybe they worshipped them here."

Theo scoffed lightly. "Worship? More like they were enslaved. Can you imagine being forced to serve those things?"

Ryu shook his head, trying to focus. "Whatever happened here, we need to find out. Let's keep moving."

As they approached the archway, a sudden chill swept through the air, causing the hairs on the back of Ryu's neck to stand on end. He paused, glancing back at his crew. "Did anyone else feel that?"

Kaida frowned, crossing her arms. "Yeah, like the temperature just dropped. It's unsettling."

Before Ryu could respond, the ground trembled beneath their feet, and a low rumble echoed through the trees. The crew exchanged nervous glances as a shadow loomed over them, blocking the fading sunlight.

"What now?" Zeno muttered, his hand tightening around his sword.

Then, from behind the archway, a massive figure emerged—an ancient guardian adorned in armor made of twisted metal and adorned with the same serpent motifs. Its eyes glowed a menacing green, and it towered over them, almost as tall as the trees surrounding them.

"Who dares trespass on sacred ground?" the guardian boomed, its voice echoing like thunder.

Ryu stepped forward, trying to keep his voice steady. "We seek the source of the light. We mean no harm."

The guardian's eyes narrowed. "The light you seek is a beacon of power. Many have come for it, but few have returned. State your purpose, or leave this place!"

Luna took a step back, her grip on her daggers tightening. "This isn't good. What if it decides we're a threat?"

Ryu glanced back at his crew, determination shining in his eyes. "We can't back down now. We've come too far."

Zeno raised an eyebrow, an almost challenging smirk on his face. "So, what do we do? Reason with it?"

The guardian tilted its head, clearly unimpressed. "You think words will save you? Show me your strength, and I will judge whether you are worthy."

With a sudden roar, the guardian lunged forward, swinging its massive arm toward Ryu and the crew. Ryu barely had time to react as he dodged to the side, shouting, "Get back!"

The impact of the guardian's swing created a shockwave, sending dust and debris flying in all directions. Zeno was quick to react, his sword drawn and gleaming. "We've got to fight back!"

"Right!" Ryu yelled, channeling his energy as he prepared to counter. "Stay together!"

Luna darted to the side, her daggers glinting in the light as she leaped at the guardian's exposed flank. "I'll distract it! Zeno, get in close!"

Zeno nodded, charging forward as he leapt alongside Luna, their movements synchronized. "We need to strike fast before it can react!"

The guardian twisted its body, narrowly avoiding Luna's attack and swinging its massive fist at Zeno. But Zeno was already on the move, slashing at the guardian's arm and creating a spark as his blade met metal.

"Not bad!" Zeno shouted, exhilaration coursing through him. "But it's going to take more than that to bring this guy down!"

Ryu, finding his footing, unleashed a powerful kick that connected with the guardian's knee. The giant stumbled slightly but quickly regained its balance, glaring down at the crew with unyielding intensity. "You fight well, but you will not defeat me with mere strength alone."

"Then we'll use our teamwork!" Kaida shouted, taking a step forward. "We're not just here for a fight. We want answers!"

The guardian hesitated for a moment, its fierce expression faltering. "Answers? Few seek knowledge; most seek power."

"Power is meaningless without understanding!" Ryu yelled, standing tall. "We're here to end the cycle of fear and violence! Let us pass, and we promise to uncover the truth behind this island."

The guardian paused, its green eyes flickering with something—curiosity, perhaps. "You would challenge the unknown for the sake of truth? Very well. Prove your resolve, and I may consider your request."

Luna, breathless from her previous efforts, looked at Ryu. "What do we do now?"

Ryu took a deep breath, feeling the energy within him stirring. "We show him who we are."

With a renewed sense of purpose, Ryu called out, "Together!"

The crew formed a line, ready to take on the guardian as a unified force. Ryu stepped forward, channeling the power within him, preparing to unlock the potential that had saved him before.

"Let's do this!" he shouted, his voice echoing through the ancient trees as the crew sprang into action, determined to prove their worth and uncover the mysteries that lay ahead.

As the crew prepared to face the guardian, Ryu felt the weight of responsibility on his shoulders. This wasn't just a battle; it was a test of their resolve, a chance to prove they were worthy of whatever secrets the island held.

"Okay, everyone, focus!" Ryu called out, scanning the determined faces of his crew. "We're not just fighting for ourselves; we're fighting for everyone who's suffered because of this island. Let's show him the strength of our bond!"

Kaida nodded fiercely, drawing her sword. "We've faced challenges before, and we've always come out stronger. We can do this together!"

Zeno grinned, his eyes sparkling with excitement. "I've got your back, Ryu! Let's show this guardian that we're more than just a bunch of misfits!"

Luna's fingers danced over her daggers, a playful smirk forming on her lips. "And if things get tough, I can always distract him with my charming personality!"

Theo chuckled, readying himself for action. "Charming? You? I'd rather rely on your knives, but I appreciate the effort!"

With their spirits high, Ryu felt a surge of energy flowing through him. He concentrated, channeling that power as the guardian prepared to charge again. "Here it comes! Get ready!"

The guardian lunged, its massive arm swinging down in a powerful arc. Ryu shouted, "Now!" as he leapt forward, using his newfound agility to dodge and roll beneath the strike.

"Zeno, now!" Ryu yelled, and Zeno darted in, slashing at the guardian's feet with precision. The blade shimmered as it connected, causing the guardian to stumble.

Luna took advantage of the opening. "You're not getting away that easily!" She leapt onto the guardian's knee, using her momentum to propel herself upward, aiming for its neck. "You'll have to do better than that!"

The guardian swatted at her, but she rolled off just in time. "You're a lot slower than you look!" she taunted, her heart racing.

Ryu seized the moment, gathering energy once again. "Now's our chance! Everyone, together!" He felt the power building within him, and he knew this was their opportunity to turn the tide.

Kaida raised her sword high, rallying the crew. "Let's combine our strength! This is our moment!"

"Right!" Theo boomed, rushing forward with his massive fists ready to deliver a blow. "For the crew!"

As they coordinated their attack, Ryu focused on channeling their combined energy. "This is it! We're stronger together!"

With synchronized movements, they all struck the guardian in unison. Zeno slashed, Luna aimed for its neck, Theo delivered a powerful punch, and Kaida thrust her sword forward. The guardian, overwhelmed by their combined assault, staggered backward.

"Impressive," it said, its voice deeper than before. "But do you have the will to continue?"

Ryu grinned, a surge of adrenaline coursing through him. "We won't back down! Not now!"

"Not until we learn the truth!" Luna shouted, her eyes fierce with determination.

"Keep pushing!" Zeno urged, stepping back to catch his breath. "We're close!"

The guardian shook its head, its eyes narrowing as if it were assessing them. "You possess great spirit. But spirit alone does not guarantee victory."

With that, it gathered energy, its body glowing as it summoned a wave of force that knocked the crew back, sending them sprawling onto the ground.

"Ryu!" Kaida cried, struggling to her feet. "We can't give up!"

Ryu pushed himself up, feeling the weight of exhaustion creeping in but refusing to relent. "We won't! We've come too far to stop now!"

"Remember what we're fighting for," Zeno added, wiping blood from his brow. "We stand together, or we fall apart!"

Ryu's resolve hardened. He felt the warmth of camaraderie filling him. "You're right. This is for everyone who's been hurt. We have to show him our true strength!"

As they regrouped, Ryu called on the energy within him, focusing it into a brilliant light that enveloped his fists. "Let's finish this!"

"Together!" they shouted in unison, rallying their strength one last time.

They charged forward, their combined energy surging as they leapt into the air. Ryu led the charge, focusing all his power into a single punch aimed at the guardian's core. "This is for everyone!"

The guardian raised its arms to defend, but Ryu's strike broke through its defenses. Light erupted from the impact, illuminating the surrounding area. The ground shook as the force of their combined attack sent shockwaves through the air.

The guardian staggered back, its eyes widening in surprise. "You truly are stronger than I anticipated!" it roared, its voice echoing through the trees. "But can you endure the consequences?"

As the dust settled, Ryu and his crew stood firm, breathing heavily but united. "We won't back down," Ryu said, looking defiantly at the guardian. "We'll keep fighting for what's right!"

The guardian paused, contemplating the spirit of the crew before it. "You have shown me strength and unity. Very well. You have proven yourselves worthy of the knowledge that lies ahead."

The tension in the air shifted, and the guardian's fierce expression softened slightly. "If you seek the light, you must first navigate the trials of this island. Only then will you uncover the truth."

Luna let out a breath she didn't know she was holding. "Trials? What kind of trials?"

The guardian pointed toward the heart of the island. "You must face the shadows of the past. Only through understanding can you hope to change the future."

Ryu nodded, feeling the weight of the guardian's words. "We'll face whatever it takes. Together."

The guardian stepped aside, allowing them to pass through the archway. "Go forth, brave adventurers. May your resolve guide you."

As the crew moved deeper into the island, a sense of purpose filled them. Each step resonated with their shared determination to uncover the truth and protect those who couldn't protect themselves.

"Whatever lies ahead," Ryu declared, "we'll face it together. Let's uncover the secrets of this island and put an end to the darkness!"

With that, the crew ventured forward, united in purpose and ready to confront whatever trials awaited them.

As Ryu led the crew deeper into the heart of the island, the atmosphere grew more intense. The lush greenery gave way to an expansive clearing where ancient ruins sprawled out before them. Massive stone pillars, adorned with intricate carvings, rose like sentinels, casting long shadows in the waning light.

"Wow, look at this place!" Kaida exclaimed, her eyes wide with awe. "It's like stepping into a forgotten world."

Zeno stepped forward, brushing his fingers along the carvings. "These designs... they tell a story. It's like a history etched in stone." He turned to Ryu, excitement bubbling in his voice. "Do you think they'll help us understand the trials we have to face?"

Ryu nodded, feeling a mix of apprehension and curiosity. "I hope so. Whatever we're up against, we need all the knowledge we can get."

Luna examined the surroundings, her eyes narrowing. "Something feels off, though. It's too quiet. I don't trust this place."

Theo chuckled, trying to lighten the mood. "What's wrong with a little quiet? Just think of it as a nice change from all the chaos we usually face!"

"Yeah, well, chaos has a way of finding us," Kaida replied, glancing over her shoulder. "I'd rather be prepared for anything."

As they stepped further into the clearing, the ground trembled again, this time more subtly, as if the very island was alive beneath their feet. Ryu looked around, sensing a shift in energy. "Everyone, stay alert. We don't know what's coming."

Suddenly, a low rumble echoed through the ruins, and a dark mist began to seep from the shadows between the pillars. It coalesced into shapes, forming eerie silhouettes that swirled and writhed as if alive.

Luna drew her daggers, her expression turning serious. "What are those? Are they... spirits?"

"Or guardians of the trials," Ryu speculated, taking a defensive stance. "Whatever they are, we have to be ready!"

The mist thickened, and from it emerged a voice—deep and resonant, echoing off the stone walls. "Brave souls who seek the truth, you must confront the shadows of your past. Only then will you be deemed worthy."

"Confront our past?" Zeno asked, frowning. "What does that even mean?"

The silhouettes began to take form, revealing figures from their pasts—friends and foes alike. Ryu's eyes widened as he saw a familiar face: his mentor, a man he had admired but had lost long ago.

"Ryu..." the apparition spoke, its voice a haunting echo of the past. "Have you truly grown stronger? Or will you repeat your mistakes?"

Ryu clenched his fists, a mixture of anger and sadness flooding through him. "I've learned from my mistakes! I won't let my past define me!"

Kaida stepped forward, her own shadow morphing into a representation of her childhood, a time when she had been powerless. "I won't let fear hold me back anymore!" she declared, raising her sword. "I've fought too hard to let my past drag me down!"

Luna found herself facing a version of herself that had once been overwhelmed with self-doubt. "You're nothing but a shadow!" she shouted, her voice filled with determination. "I'm stronger than you'll ever know!"

Theo faced an embodiment of failure, a moment when he had let his crew down. "I've learned to rise above, no matter how many times I fall!" He brandished his fists, ready to fight.

Zeno, standing tall, felt his own shadow stir. "You think you can intimidate me with memories? I'm not afraid of what I was—I'm proud of who I've become!" His sword glimmered with resolve.

As each crew member confronted their past, Ryu felt a surge of energy building among them. "Together! We can overcome this!" he shouted, looking at his friends. "We've faced down enemies and challenges far greater than mere shadows. Let's show them our true strength!"

With that, they all surged forward, ready to face the manifestations of their pasts. The shadows twisted and swirled, but the crew fought as one, their combined resolve illuminating the darkness.

"Ryu, focus!" Kaida called, slashing through her shadow. "Remember who you are! You've come so far!"

"Don't let them trick you!" Zeno shouted, parrying a strike from his shadow. "Fight back with everything you've got!"

With each blow they landed, the shadows began to dissipate, revealing the truth behind their fears and insecurities. Ryu felt a wave of clarity washing over him as he battled his own doubts. "I am not defined by my past! I am a protector, a fighter, and I will forge my own destiny!"

As the last of the shadows faded, the air grew still. The dark mist dissipated, revealing a glowing path leading deeper into the ruins. The guardian's voice returned, echoing through the clearing. "You have faced your past and emerged stronger. You are now worthy to proceed."

Ryu looked at his crew, their faces alight with determination and triumph. "We did it! We faced our fears together!"

Luna beamed, her eyes shining. "I knew we could do it! There's nothing we can't overcome if we stick together."

Theo punched the air in victory. "And there's still more to come! Let's keep pushing forward!"

Zeno grinned, his energy revitalized. "Right! Whatever lies ahead, we'll tackle it as a team."

Kaida raised her sword, a fire igniting in her eyes. "Let's find that light and uncover the truth of this island!"

As they stepped forward, the glowing path leading them deeper into the ruins, Ryu felt a renewed sense of purpose. They had faced their shadows and emerged victorious. Now, nothing could stand in their way.

"Let's go, crew! The adventure isn't over yet!" Ryu shouted, leading the way into the unknown.

As Ryu and the crew ventured deeper into the ruins, the atmosphere shifted dramatically. The air crackled with energy, and the very ground seemed to pulse beneath their feet. A grand chamber loomed ahead, its massive entrance framed by ancient stone sculptures that depicted celestial beings descending from the heavens.

"This must be it," Ryu said, his heart racing with anticipation. "The heart of the Island of Ascension."

"Look at those carvings," Kaida pointed out, tracing the intricate designs with her fingers. "They're beautiful, but they also seem... ominous."

Zeno squinted at the sculptures. "They depict the god of this island. I've heard legends about him—an entity of immense power, said to grant wisdom and strength to those who prove themselves worthy."

Luna crossed her arms, her expression thoughtful. "And punish those who fail. I hope we're ready for whatever we're about to face."

Theo chuckled nervously. "If he's anything like the guardians we've faced, I'm sure he'll be a handful!"

As they entered the chamber, a soft, ethereal light enveloped them, casting flickering shadows on the walls. At the center of the room stood a pedestal, upon which rested a shimmering orb that pulsed with a radiant energy.

"Is that...?" Ryu began, his eyes widening.

"Must be the heart of the island," Zeno concluded. "We need to approach carefully."

As they stepped forward, a deep voice resonated throughout the chamber, echoing off the stone walls. "Who dares to disturb the sanctity of the Island of Ascension?"

The crew froze, scanning their surroundings. "Show yourself!" Ryu called out, his voice steady despite the unease creeping in.

From the shadows, a figure emerged—a tall, imposing presence adorned in robes that shimmered like stars. His hair flowed like liquid silver, and his eyes glowed with a celestial light. "I am Orpheon, the god of this island," he proclaimed, his voice powerful yet calm. "State your purpose."

Ryu took a step forward, his heart pounding. "We've come to seek your wisdom and uncover the truth of this island. We want to protect those who cannot protect themselves."

Orpheon regarded him with a piercing gaze. "And what makes you worthy of my wisdom? Many have sought my guidance, yet few have proven themselves."

Kaida squared her shoulders, determination etched on her face. "We've faced our fears, battled shadows from our pasts, and stood united against overwhelming odds. We're not just a crew; we're a family."

"And families fight for each other," Zeno added, stepping beside her. "We've come too far to turn back now. We won't let anything stop us!"

Luna nodded vigorously. "We've sacrificed too much for this. We're ready to face whatever trials you set before us."

Orpheon's expression remained unreadable, but the energy in the room shifted subtly. "Very well. You speak with conviction. But words alone will not suffice. You must prove your resolve through a trial of strength and spirit."

Theo glanced at Ryu, a mix of excitement and apprehension in his eyes. "What kind of trial?"

Orpheon raised his hand, and the orb on the pedestal flared brightly. "You will face the Trials of Ascendance. Each of you will confront your deepest fears and demonstrate your strength. Only then will I grant you the knowledge you seek."

Ryu exchanged glances with his crew. "We're ready for whatever you throw at us!"

"Bring it on!" Kaida exclaimed, her confidence unwavering.

"Yeah! We've handled worse!" Zeno added with a grin.

Orpheon nodded slowly, the light from the orb swirling in response to their resolve. "Very well. Prepare yourselves."

The chamber transformed around them, the walls dissolving into a swirling mist. Ryu felt a rush of energy as the environment shifted, and he found himself standing alone on a desolate battlefield, surrounded by echoes of past battles.

"Ryu!" a voice called out, familiar yet haunting. He turned to see his mentor standing before him, a disappointed expression on his face. "You've come back to face your failures?"

Ryu clenched his fists, feeling the weight of his past mistakes crashing over him. "No! I'm not here to dwell on the past. I'm here to prove I've changed!"

His mentor shook his head. "But have you really? You've lost so much, Ryu. Will you let your fears consume you once more?"

"Not this time!" Ryu shouted, channeling his energy. "I've learned from my mistakes. I fight for my crew, for those who can't fight for themselves!"

As the battlefield began to shift around him, he felt the presence of his friends nearby, each facing their own trials. He could hear their voices, echoing through the chaos.

"Ryu! Remember who you are!" Kaida's voice rang out, filled with conviction.

"Focus on your strength!" Zeno encouraged, his own battle raging in the background.

Luna shouted, "We believe in you! Don't let the past win!"

Fueled by their support, Ryu felt his resolve solidify. "I won't be defeated by my past! I am stronger than my fears!"

He charged forward, determined to break free from the shadow of doubt, ready to face whatever lay ahead. The battlefield transformed into a bright arena, and as he stood tall, the mist began to dissipate, revealing his true strength.

"I will prove myself, not just to you, but to everyone who has ever doubted me!" Ryu declared, feeling the power of his crew behind him.

And in that moment, he knew he was ready to face whatever trials awaited him, united with his friends, determined to uncover the truth of the Island of Ascension.

As Ryu stood resolute in the glowing arena, the ethereal energy crackled around him. Suddenly, the air shimmered, and Orpheon reappeared, standing tall with an enigmatic smile.

"Impressive," the god said, his voice echoing like distant thunder. "You have a fire within you, Ryu. But the trials are far from over. Each of you must confront your fears, not only in spirit but in combat. Are you ready to face what lies ahead?"

Ryu nodded firmly, his determination unwavering. "We're ready. Whatever you throw at us, we'll face it together."

Orpheon raised an eyebrow, intrigued. "Very well. Each trial will test not only your strength but the bonds you share. True power comes from unity."

With a wave of his hand, the arena shifted again, swirling into darkness. The crew found themselves standing in a vast expanse filled with towering shadows, each one representing a different fear or challenge they had faced.

"Look!" Kaida pointed, her voice steady. "These shadows... they're reflections of our past battles!"

"More like our insecurities," Luna added, eyes narrowed as she scanned the looming figures. "We need to stick together. If we let them divide us, we'll lose."

"Right! Remember, we're stronger as a team!" Theo shouted, clenching his fists in determination. "Let's take these shadows down!"

"Stay focused!" Zeno called, his sword glinting in the dim light. "If we work together, we can conquer anything!"

As they gathered, Orpheon's voice echoed through the darkness. "To conquer your fears, you must fight not only the shadows but the doubts they bring. Who will face the first trial?"

"I will!" Ryu stepped forward, feeling the weight of expectation. "I've faced my past before, and I won't let it hold me back now!"

Orpheon nodded, and the shadows around them began to coalesce, forming into a familiar figure: Ryu's mentor, appearing just as he remembered, disappointment etched on his face.

"Ryu," the shadow spoke, its voice a haunting echo. "Have you truly learned from your past? Or are you destined to repeat your mistakes?"

"I've learned!" Ryu shouted back, his voice steady. "I've lost so much, but I fight for my crew now. I won't let you drag me down!"

With a fierce determination, he lunged at the shadow, ready to prove that he had grown beyond his past. The moment he struck, the shadow dissipated into wisps of darkness, only to reform behind him, relentless.

"Your strength alone won't save you, Ryu," it taunted. "You must learn to rely on others, or you will fall!"

At that moment, the crew rallied around him. "Ryu, we're here!" Kaida called, her voice cutting through the tension. "You're not alone!"

"Fight for us!" Zeno encouraged, his eyes shining with support. "We believe in you!"

Luna added, "Let us face this together! You don't have to carry the weight alone!"

Fueled by their words, Ryu turned to face the shadow once more. "You're right! I've tried to bear everything on my own, but that's not how strength works. I have my crew, and together, we're unstoppable!"

As he declared this, the shadows around him shifted, forming into a swirling mass that began to echo the faces of his friends. "Together," they whispered, and Ryu felt a surge of power course through him.

Orpheon watched with a knowing smile, his eyes gleaming with approval. "Now you understand. The bonds you share are your greatest weapon."

With newfound determination, Ryu focused his energy, channeling the support of his friends. "Let's finish this!" he yelled, launching into a flurry of powerful strikes, empowered not just by his strength but by the unity of his crew.

As the shadow began to falter, the others prepared to face their own trials, each ready to confront their fears with the strength of their bonds. Kaida stepped forward next, her own shadow looming large—a representation of her past failures and insecurities.

"I'm not afraid!" she declared, drawing her sword. "I've fought too hard to let fear take me down again!"

Zeno nodded, standing beside her. "We'll fight with you, Kaida. No one faces their shadows alone!"

Orpheon raised his hand, and the shadows shifted to reveal Kaida's trial—a fierce opponent who mirrored her past struggles. "Face your doubts, Kaida. Show me your true strength."

As each crew member took their turn facing their shadows, the air filled with the sound of clashing steel and shouts of encouragement. Ryu could see how the trials were molding them, pushing them to grow even stronger together.

"Remember, you're never alone!" he shouted, channeling his energy into his next strike.

The trials continued, and as each friend fought their shadows, Ryu could feel the presence of Orpheon watching, observing their growth. With every victory, the shadows weakened, and the bonds among the crew grew even tighter.

As the last shadow fell, the chamber erupted in light, illuminating the path to the heart of the island. Orpheon stood before them, his expression filled with pride.

"You have faced your fears and emerged victorious," he proclaimed, his voice booming like thunder. "You are truly worthy of the wisdom of the Island of Ascension."

The crew exchanged glances filled with exhilaration and relief. "What's next?" Theo asked, his excitement palpable.

Orpheon gestured toward the glowing orb behind him. "The heart of this island holds knowledge and power beyond your imagination. Approach, and let it guide you on your journey."

Ryu stepped forward, his heart racing. "We're ready. Let's uncover the truth and prepare for whatever comes next!"

As they moved toward the orb, Ryu felt a surge of hope. With his friends by his side, he knew they could face any challenge that lay ahead. The adventure was just beginning, and together, they would uncover the secrets of the Island of Ascension.

As Ryu and the crew approached the radiant orb, the air around them shimmered with an electric anticipation. The orb pulsed with vibrant colors, casting a mesmerizing glow that illuminated their faces.

"Look at it!" Luna exclaimed, her eyes wide with wonder. "It's beautiful! I can feel the energy radiating from it."

"I've never seen anything like it," Kaida said, stepping closer, her hand reaching out instinctively. "It's like it's calling to us."

Zeno kept his sword at the ready, scanning the area for any potential threats. "We need to be cautious. This orb might hold incredible power, but it could also come with a price."

Ryu nodded, his heart racing. "Whatever it is, we'll face it together. We've come too far to turn back now."

Orpheon stepped aside, allowing them access to the orb. "The heart of the Island of Ascension is a repository of knowledge, strength, and the wisdom of those who have come before you. Approach with open hearts and minds, and it will reveal what you seek."

As Ryu reached out, he felt a warm, inviting energy envelop his hand. The moment his fingers made contact with the orb, a surge of memories flooded his mind—visions of past heroes, their struggles, and triumphs echoing through time.

"Ryu, what do you see?" Kaida asked, concern etched on her face.

"It's incredible," Ryu breathed, his voice barely above a whisper. "I can see the battles fought for justice, the sacrifices made for the sake of others... and the bonds formed in the heat of conflict. It's all here."

"Don't get lost in it!" Zeno warned, his eyes narrowing. "We need to stay focused."

Suddenly, the orb began to vibrate more intensely, and the colors shifted rapidly. "Ryu, focus on what we need!" Luna urged, her voice breaking through the mesmerizing visions. "What do we need to know to fight the Executioners?"

As if responding to her words, the orb's light brightened, and a new vision emerged—a landscape marred by chaos, with figures clad in dark armor wreaking havoc. Ryu's heart sank as he recognized the Executioners, their ruthless leader Goran looming ominously in the background.

"Look!" Ryu shouted, pointing toward the vision. "That's where they're attacking! We have to warn the villagers!"

"Yes!" Kaida exclaimed, her determination rekindled. "We can't let them suffer! We have to rally everyone and fight back!"

"But first," Orpheon interjected, his voice grave, "you must understand the true nature of your adversaries. The Executioners are not just warriors; they are driven by their own fears and desires. To defeat them, you must expose their weaknesses."

Ryu turned back to the orb, feeling its energy pulse through him. "How do we do that? How can we find their weaknesses?"

"By embracing your own," Orpheon replied. "Each of you must confront your past and emerge stronger. Only then will you gain the insight needed to understand and combat your foes."

Theo clenched his fists, determination written across his face. "Then let's do it! We'll face our pasts again if it means protecting others."

"I'll go first," Zeno volunteered, stepping forward. "I need to confront what holds me back. If I'm going to protect my friends, I can't let fear dictate my actions."

With that, Zeno reached toward the orb, and it glowed even brighter, enveloping him in a radiant light. The chamber shifted once more, transforming into a shadowy forest filled with echoes of laughter and cries of despair.

"Zeno!" Kaida shouted, but Orpheon held up a hand.

"Let him face his trial. We will be here to support him."

As the scene settled, Zeno found himself standing before an old version of himself—one who had given in to despair and lost hope in the fight against the darkness. The figure pointed accusingly, his voice filled with bitterness. "You think you can change? You were weak then, and you're weak now!"

"I'm not weak!" Zeno shouted, his voice strong. "I've faced my fears! I've fought alongside my friends, and I've learned from my mistakes!"

The shadow of his former self laughed mockingly. "But what will you do when it really matters? Will you abandon them, just like you abandoned your dreams?"

"I won't abandon anyone!" Zeno declared fiercely. "I fight for my friends, for those who can't fight for themselves! You don't define me!"

With that proclamation, Zeno unleashed a surge of energy, and the shadow wavered, flickering like a candle in the wind. The forest around him began to dissolve as the light from the orb intensified.

"Keep pushing!" Ryu called, his voice echoing in the distance. "You can do this!"

Zeno focused, channeling the energy of his friends, their support bolstering his resolve. "I am not defined by my past! I choose my path, and I choose to stand with my crew!"

As Zeno struck the shadow, it shattered into a million fragments, dissipating into the air. The chamber erupted in light, and Zeno found himself back with the crew, breathless but triumphant.

"You did it!" Kaida cheered, her eyes sparkling with pride.

"I faced my fears, and it felt amazing," Zeno said, a grin spreading across his face. "Now it's time for the rest of us to do the same!"

Orpheon nodded approvingly. "You have begun to understand. Who will step forward next?"

"I will," Luna said, her voice steady despite the anxiety in her heart. "It's time for me to confront what holds me back."

As she stepped toward the orb, Ryu felt a sense of solidarity among them. "We believe in you, Luna! You've got this!"

The orb pulsed, and as Luna touched it, the chamber transformed once again, revealing a vast ocean filled with crashing waves and swirling storms. In the distance, she could see a figure drowning, a reflection of her fears—her insecurities about her strength and ability to protect her friends.

"No!" Luna shouted, rushing forward. "I won't let fear control me!"

But the figure, a shadowy version of herself, rose from the water, its voice echoing with doubt. "You're not strong enough. You've always held back, afraid to unleash your true power."

"I'm not afraid anymore!" Luna declared, summoning her energy. "I will protect my friends, no matter what!"

As she channeled her power, the storm around her began to calm, and the shadow faltered. "You think you can change the tides? You will fail, just like you always do!"

"Not this time!" Luna shouted, drawing strength from her crew's unwavering support. "I am not alone! Together, we can overcome anything!"

With a powerful surge, Luna unleashed a wave of energy, crashing against the shadow. The storm shattered, revealing the calm waters of her heart, and the shadow dissipated into nothingness.

"You did it!" Ryu exclaimed as she rejoined the crew, her expression radiant.

"I faced my fears, and I feel... free," Luna said, her voice filled with awe.

Orpheon looked pleased. "You are all progressing beautifully. The trials will only grow tougher, but together, you can conquer anything."

"Who's next?" Theo asked, stepping forward with determination. "I'm ready to face whatever comes my way!"

As he reached for the orb, Ryu couldn't help but feel a sense of pride for his crew. Each of them was finding their strength, proving that the bonds they shared were their greatest weapon.

"Let's keep this going!" Kaida shouted, her enthusiasm infectious. "We'll face everything together, just like we always do!"

And with that, the trials continued, each crew member stepping forward to confront their shadows, uncovering their strengths and fears while the heart of the Island of Ascension awaited to share its wisdom. Together, they would forge a path forward, ready to face the Executioners and protect those who could not protect themselves.

As the crew gathered around the glowing orb, the air hummed with energy. Ryu could feel the anticipation buzzing among them, but he knew they needed more than just strength; they needed information.

"Okay, everyone," Ryu began, his voice steady. "We've faced our fears and grown stronger. Now we need to figure out where the Executioners are hiding so we can put an end to their chaos."

Luna nodded, her expression serious. "We can't just charge in blindly. We need to know their plans, their numbers, and where they're based. The orb showed us their power, but we need more details."

Kaida crossed her arms, her brow furrowing in thought. "I overheard some villagers talking about a fortress in the mountains. They said it's heavily guarded and surrounded by a treacherous landscape. If the Executioners are using it as their base, we'll have to be strategic in our approach."

"Do we have any allies we can call on?" Zeno asked, looking around at the crew. "We might need more than just the five of us if we're going to take on the Executioners in their own territory."

Ryu clenched his fists, determination rising within him. "We've made friends along the way. We should reach out to anyone willing to help us. But first, we need to confirm the location of their headquarters."

Orpheon stepped forward, his presence commanding attention. "I can assist you with this. The orb contains not only the heart of this island but also echoes of the past. If you wish, I can help you focus your energy to reveal the Executioners' headquarters."

"Please do!" Theo said, excitement bubbling in his voice. "We can't let them continue terrorizing people!"

Orpheon nodded, raising his hands toward the orb. "Gather your energy, and focus on the images you've seen. The knowledge you seek is within your grasp."

As they concentrated, the orb began to shimmer and pulse, displaying flickering images of the Executioners' fortress—a dark, imposing structure perched on a mountain ledge, surrounded by thick forests and steep cliffs. Guards patrolled the walls, and ominous shadows flitted about, hinting at the threats lurking within.

"There it is!" Ryu exclaimed, pointing at the image. "That's their headquarters!"

Kaida squinted at the details. "It looks heavily fortified. We'll need to be cautious if we're going to infiltrate it."

"Look at the layout," Zeno noted, tracing the map with his finger. "There are entry points that might be less guarded. If we're smart about this, we can slip in unnoticed."

Luna stepped closer to the orb, her eyes narrowing as she examined the shifting images. "What if we create a diversion? If we can draw some of the guards away, it might give us the opening we need."

Ryu's eyes lit up with realization. "That's a great idea! We could set something off on the opposite side of the fortress. It'll give us a chance to slip in and locate Kaida."

"The villagers could help us," Kaida suggested. "If we explain what we're doing, they might be willing to assist. They know the area better than we do."

Theo nodded enthusiastically. "We can rally everyone and plan our attack. But first, we need to know how many allies we can gather. We can't take on the Executioners alone."

"Let's split up," Ryu proposed. "Kaida, Zeno, and I will go to the village and talk to the people. Luna and Theo, you can scout the area around the fortress and gather intel on the guards and their routines."

"Got it!" Luna replied, determination shining in her eyes. "We'll find out everything we can about their defenses."

"And we'll return with news of our allies," Kaida added, her voice steady. "We need to be ready for anything."

As they prepared to split up, Orpheon offered one last piece of advice. "Remember, the strength of your bonds will carry you through. Trust one another and fight as a united front."

With that, the crew set off in their respective directions, each feeling the weight of their mission. As Ryu, Kaida, and Zeno made their way to the village, the tension hung in the air like a storm cloud, but their resolve was unshakable.

Arriving at the village, they were met with wary glances from the villagers, but Kaida stepped forward confidently. "We're here to help! The Executioners are a threat to all of us, and we need your support."

An elder approached, her expression a mix of skepticism and curiosity. "You think you can take on the Executioners? They've been a scourge on our land for too long."

Ryu stepped in, his voice earnest. "We can't do it alone, but together, we have a chance. We've faced them before, and we've grown stronger. If we join forces, we can protect our homes."

The elder considered their words, glancing back at the other villagers, who whispered among themselves. "What proof do you have that you can succeed?"

Zeno chimed in, raising his sword. "We've defeated their guards before. We know their tactics. If you trust us, we can take the fight to them and liberate this village."

The elder's eyes narrowed, searching for sincerity. "Very well. If you truly believe you can make a difference, we'll support you. But you must show us you are worthy."

"Let us prove ourselves," Kaida said, determination in her voice. "We'll set up a plan to attack their fortress, and we'll need your people to help spread the word. Gather whoever is willing to fight!"

As the villagers nodded and began to murmur in agreement, Ryu felt a surge of hope. "Together, we'll drive the Executioners from this land!"

Meanwhile, Luna and Theo had ventured to the cliffs overlooking the fortress, peering down at the guards moving methodically along the walls.

"Look at that!" Theo pointed. "They're using the same routes over and over. If we time it right, we can sneak in undetected."

Luna nodded, taking note of the guards' movements. "We'll need to act quickly. Once we gather enough allies, we can create a diversion on the opposite side of the fortress, drawing their attention away from the entrance."

As they observed, a commotion broke out in the courtyard below, with guards shouting and running around. "What's happening?" Theo asked, eyes wide.

"I don't know, but we should find out!" Luna replied, her heart racing. "Let's get closer!"

They moved silently along the cliffs, trying to catch glimpses of the chaos below. It was then they spotted a group of villagers trying to break into the fortress, a brave but reckless attempt to rescue loved ones taken by the Executioners.

"This could work to our advantage," Luna whispered. "If we can help them, it might create the diversion we need!"

"Right! Let's go!" Theo urged, and they climbed down the rocks, racing toward the action.

As Ryu, Kaida, and Zeno returned to the village, they found the elder surrounded by villagers, all discussing plans and strategies. The atmosphere was charged with determination.

"Everyone!" Ryu called, gathering their attention. "We've made progress. The villagers are willing to fight with us against the Executioners!"

Cheers erupted, and the elder nodded, her expression transformed from skepticism to fierce resolve. "Then let us prepare! We will not stand idly by while they terrorize our homes!"

Back at the fortress, Luna and Theo had reached the chaos, quickly devising a plan to help the villagers break in. "We need to create a distraction," Luna said, scanning the area for anything they could use.

"I can create a smoke bomb!" Theo suggested, rummaging through his bag. "If I throw it over there, it'll draw the guards away!"

"Do it!" Luna urged, her heart pounding with adrenaline.

Theo pulled out a small device and tossed it toward a nearby pile of crates. It exploded into a cloud of thick smoke, engulfing the area and causing confusion among the guards.

"Now's our chance!" Luna shouted, leading the way as they joined the villagers in their attempt to breach the fortress.

As the guards scrambled to investigate, Ryu, Kaida, and Zeno felt the momentum building back in the village. They shared determined glances, each understanding that they were on the brink of something monumental.

"Let's gather our forces and prepare for the attack!" Ryu shouted, raising his fist. "Today, we fight for our homes and for each other!"

With the promise of unity and strength, the crew forged ahead, ready to take the fight to the Executioners. The Island of Ascension would witness a battle unlike any before, as the bonds of friendship and bravery lit the way forward.

As the crew regrouped after their discussions and strategies, Ryu felt a sense of urgency in the air. The villagers were rallying behind them, but there was still a lingering uncertainty about the Executioners' true movements.

"Everyone, gather around!" Ryu called, drawing the attention of Kaida, Zeno, Luna, and Theo. They formed a tight circle, eager to hear what he had discovered. "I've been speaking with some of the villagers, and it seems there's been a change in the Executioners' plans. They're not just holed up in that fortress; they've relocated to another island."

"What?!" Kaida exclaimed, disbelief flashing across her face. "How do we know this isn't just a rumor?"

Ryu held up a hand to calm her. "I spoke to an old sailor who saw them moving supplies and weapons. He said they're setting up a stronghold on a smaller island just east of here—an island known for its treacherous waters and strange weather."

"That's not good," Zeno said, furrowing his brow. "If they're regrouping, they could be planning something big. We can't let them consolidate their power."

Luna crossed her arms, her expression serious. "We need to act fast. If we can get there before they finish setting up, we can catch them off guard."

"Exactly," Ryu agreed, his resolve strengthening. "We'll need to gather our allies and make a plan. But first, we need to find a way to navigate through those treacherous waters without drawing too much attention."

Theo chimed in, excitement bubbling in his voice. "I know the area! The waters are tricky, but there's a hidden passage through the rocks that can take us closer to the island without being detected. It's risky, but it might work!"

"Then we have a plan!" Kaida said, her eyes shining with determination. "Let's gather everyone and set sail. We don't have a moment to lose."

As they prepared to leave, Ryu felt the weight of responsibility pressing on his shoulders. The crew was counting on him, and he couldn't afford to let them down. They rallied the villagers, sharing their new intel and inspiring them to join the cause.

Once the villagers agreed to help, the crew set out toward the dock where their ship awaited. As they boarded, Ryu stood at the helm, his heart pounding with excitement and anxiety.

"Okay, everyone!" Ryu called out, looking at his crew. "We're heading east toward the Executioners' new base. Remember, this isn't just a fight for us; it's for the villagers who have suffered under their tyranny. Let's show them what we're made of!"

As the ship sailed through the waves, the air grew tense with anticipation. The crew shared stories and laughter, bolstering each other's spirits. But as they approached the island, the atmosphere shifted. The once serene waters began to churn violently, and dark clouds gathered overhead.

"Looks like the weather is turning," Zeno noted, squinting at the horizon. "We need to navigate carefully. I'll help with the sails."

Luna rushed to the side of the ship, her eyes scanning the turbulent waters. "Those waves look dangerous! We need to keep our balance and avoid capsizing!"

With Zeno managing the sails and Luna coordinating the crew, they maneuvered through the rough seas. The ship rocked violently, and Ryu gripped the helm tightly, his heart racing.

Suddenly, the ship lurched, and everyone stumbled. "Hold on!" Ryu shouted, regaining his footing. "We can't lose control now!"

The wind howled as they approached the rocky passage Theo had mentioned. "It's just ahead!" Theo called, pointing toward a narrow opening in the cliffs. "We need to steer through there!"

"Everyone, brace yourselves!" Ryu yelled, determination surging within him. "We're almost through!"

They maneuvered through the narrow passage, the cliffs towering over them like giants. Just as they emerged on the other side, a flash of lightning illuminated the sky, revealing the ominous silhouette of the Executioners' stronghold on the distant island.

"There it is!" Kaida exclaimed, her voice filled with urgency. "We made it!"

As they sailed closer, the crew could see the island more clearly. It was shrouded in mist, and the fortress loomed ominously, surrounded by guards patrolling the beaches and cliffs. The sense of danger was palpable.

"This is it," Ryu said, steeling himself. "We need to be careful. We're outnumbered, but if we use the element of surprise, we might just pull this off."

"Let's anchor here," Zeno suggested. "We can make our approach on foot. We'll scout the area and look for weaknesses."

As they secured the ship, Ryu felt a mix of excitement and dread. "Everyone, stay sharp. This is a pivotal moment for us. We've fought hard to get here, and we can't let the Executioners take our momentum."

With that, the crew disembarked, stealthily making their way toward the treeline that bordered the beach. They crept through the underbrush, their senses heightened, every sound amplified by the tense atmosphere.

"Look over there," Luna whispered, pointing to a group of guards gathered near the entrance of the fortress, seemingly relaxed. "If we can distract them, we might slip past."

Ryu nodded, formulating a plan in his mind. "Kaida, you and Zeno create a diversion. Luna and Theo, you'll follow me as we scout the perimeter."

"Got it!" Kaida replied, determination flashing in her eyes.

"Just be careful," Zeno warned. "We don't want to alert the entire base."

As they split up, Ryu felt a surge of adrenaline. This was their chance to take down the Executioners once and for all. He motioned for Luna and Theo to follow him as they carefully approached the edge of the fortress, hiding behind the thick foliage.

"Let's see what we're up against," Ryu said, peering through the leaves. The guards were still gathered, laughing and chatting, unaware of the storm brewing just outside their walls.

"We can't let this opportunity slip away," Theo whispered, eyes wide. "If we wait too long, they might notice something's off."

"Let's wait for Kaida and Zeno to create their distraction," Ryu replied, his gaze fixed on the guards. "Then we'll move in."

Moments later, a loud crash echoed from the other side of the fortress. Ryu's heart raced as he turned to see a plume of smoke rising into the air, followed by the frantic shouts of the guards.

"Now!" Ryu shouted, rushing forward. "This is our chance!"

They darted toward the fortress, adrenaline pumping through their veins. As they approached the entrance, Ryu could see the guards scrambling to respond to the disturbance, their attention diverted.

"Let's go!" Luna urged, and they slipped through the entrance, hearts pounding.

Inside, the atmosphere shifted. The air was thick with tension and the smell of sweat. Ryu exchanged glances with his crew, silently affirming their resolve. They had come too far to turn back now.

"Stay alert," Ryu whispered as they crept down a dimly lit corridor. "We need to find their command center. That's where we can gather intel and maybe even disrupt their plans."

Suddenly, they heard footsteps approaching. Ryu pressed himself against the wall, motioning for the others to do the same. A pair of guards walked by, chatting casually, completely oblivious to the storm brewing just behind them.

"Can you believe what happened at the last raid?" one guard said, laughing. "Those fools thought they could sneak past us! It was too easy!"

"Yeah, but the boss is getting restless," the other guard replied. "He wants to see more action. We need to tighten security."

Ryu's heart sank at their words. "They're planning something big," he whispered to his crew. "We have to stop them."

Once the guards were out of earshot, Ryu turned to Luna and Theo. "We need to find a map or something that shows their plans. If they're getting ready to strike again, we have to know where and when."

Luna nodded, her eyes sharp with focus. "Let's keep moving."

They pressed deeper into the fortress, navigating through dimly lit hallways and avoiding guards as they went. Finally, they stumbled upon a large room filled with maps and documents spread across a central table.

"This is it!" Ryu exclaimed, rushing to the table. He began scanning the maps, searching for any indication of the Executioners' next move. "If we can find out where they're planning their next raid, we can warn the villagers."

"Look at this!" Theo shouted, pointing to a map that detailed their movements across the islands. "They've got a schedule for attacks! They're hitting multiple villages at once!"

Kaida's eyes widened as she joined them. "We need to take this back with us. This is crucial information!"

Just as they began to gather the documents, the door burst open, and a group of guards stormed in. "Intruders!" one shouted, drawing his sword. "Get them!"

"Run!" Ryu shouted, grabbing the maps. "We can't let them catch us!"

They dashed out of the room, adrenaline pumping through their veins as they raced down the hallway. Behind them, the sounds of chaos erupted as the guards began to mobilize.

"Split up!" Kaida shouted, leading the way down a side corridor. "We can confuse them!"

Ryu nodded, urgency coursing through him. "We'll meet back at the entrance. Stay safe!"

As they scattered, Ryu's heart raced. He could hear the guards shouting, their footsteps echoing through the fortress. They needed to escape with the information, and fast.

He ducked into a nearby room, hiding behind a stack of crates. The guards ran past, their voices filled with anger and frustration. "They can't have gone far! Spread out!"

Once they were out of sight, Ryu slipped out of the room and made his way toward the exit, clutching the maps tightly. As he reached the entrance, he spotted Luna and Theo waiting anxiously.

"Where's Kaida and Zeno?" Luna asked, worry etched on her face.

"I don't know!" Ryu replied, scanning the area. "We need to get out of here before they catch us!"

Just then, a loud explosion shook the ground, and the entrance collapsed in a cloud of dust and debris. "They're onto us!" Theo shouted, panic rising.

"Quick, we need another way out!" Ryu urged, pushing forward as the chaos unfolded around them. The fortress was coming alive with guards, and they had to find a way to escape.

They darted through the crumbling hallways, desperate to find an exit. As they reached a side door, they spotted Zeno and Kaida rushing toward them, breathless but determined.

"Ryu!" Kaida called, relief flooding her voice. "We were looking for you! We need to go, now!"

"Follow me!" Ryu shouted, leading them through the side door just as more guards poured into the hallway.

Outside, the night was alive with chaos. The crew raced across the beach, the sound of their footsteps mingling with the distant shouts of the guards behind them.

"We have to reach the ship!" Zeno yelled, glancing back at the fortress. "They'll be right behind us!"

As they sprinted toward the water, Ryu felt the adrenaline coursing through his veins. They were so close, but he knew they couldn't stop now. "Keep moving! We're almost there!"

Just as they reached the shoreline, Ryu turned to see the guards emerging from the fortress, their faces twisted in fury. "Stop them!" one guard shouted, pointing at the crew.

"Get on the ship!" Ryu yelled, urgency in his voice. "We'll hold them off!"

Kaida shook her head. "No way! We stick together!"

Luna nodded, determination shining in her eyes. "We'll fight!"

As the guards closed in, Ryu felt a surge of courage. "We're not backing down! This ends here!"

With that, the crew readied themselves for the confrontation, standing together as a united front against the forces of the Executioners. They were prepared to fight for their freedom, their friends, and the future of the islands they held dear.

As the crew braced themselves for the impending clash, a sudden, eerie silence descended over the beach. Before they could react, a blinding light enveloped them. They instinctively shielded their eyes, but it was too late. The guards had unleashed a strange power, summoning translucent bubbles that surrounded each crew member.

"What is this?!" Ryu shouted, struggling against the shimmering prison. He could feel a strange energy sapping his strength, the world around him fading as he fought to stay conscious.

"Ryu! Fight it!" Kaida cried, her own bubble encasing her. "We can't let them take us!"

"Don't give up!" Zeno added, straining against the confinement. But one by one, their voices began to fade, replaced by an overwhelming sense of drowsiness. Ryu could see the outlines of his crew growing blurry, their movements becoming sluggish.

"Stay awake! Stay—" Ryu's words trailed off as darkness enveloped him, and he succumbed to the powerful force pulling him under.

When Ryu finally opened his eyes, the familiar sights of his crew and the beach were gone. Instead, he found himself lying on soft sand, the sun beating down on him. He sat up, confusion swirling in his mind. "Where... where am I?"

He scanned his surroundings and realized he was on a completely different island, lush with vibrant greenery and towering trees. The sound of waves crashing against the shore filled the air, but there was no sign of his crew. Panic set in. "Kaida! Zeno! Luna! Theo!" he called out, but only silence answered him.

As he stood, a figure emerged from the trees—a tall man dressed in bright tribal attire, adorned with feathers and shells. His face bore a serious expression, and he approached Ryu with caution.

"Who are you?" Ryu demanded, still disoriented. "What happened to my crew?"

The man paused, assessing Ryu before speaking. "You've arrived at the Island of Lost Echoes. The Executioners have dispersed your group across different islands, trapping each of you in a magical bubble."

"Magical bubble?" Ryu echoed, anger igniting within him. "We have to get back to our friends!"

"Getting back is not easy," the man said, his tone grave. "Each island has its own trials, and you must face them alone to reunite with your crew."

Ryu clenched his fists, determination boiling inside him. "I'm not leaving my friends behind. I'll find a way to reunite with them, no matter what it takes!"

The man nodded slowly, respect glimmering in his eyes. "Then you must prove yourself. Each trial will test your strength, your heart, and your resolve. Only then will you earn the path back to your friends."

"Tell me what I need to do!" Ryu urged, ready for whatever challenge lay ahead.

"The first trial lies beyond the forest, at the Temple of Echoes," the man explained. "You must retrieve the Crystal of Harmony from its depths. But be warned, many have tried and failed. The echoes of the past can lead you astray."

Ryu's mind raced. He was alone, but he couldn't let fear deter him. "I'll do it. I won't let my crew down."

As he set off toward the forest, Ryu's heart pounded with a mix of fear and resolve. He pushed through the dense underbrush, the sounds of the island amplifying around him. The air felt electric, charged with possibilities.

After what felt like hours, Ryu reached the entrance of the Temple of Echoes, its grand structure looming before him, adorned with intricate carvings and vines. Taking a deep breath, he stepped inside, the air cool and dark.

Inside the temple, shadows danced across the walls, and whispers echoed through the chambers. Ryu paused, his instincts kicking in. "Focus," he muttered to himself. "It's just an echo."

As he ventured deeper, he spotted the Crystal of Harmony glowing faintly at the center of the main chamber, surrounded by a shimmering pool of water. But as he approached, a voice resonated through the temple, rich and melodic.

"Who dares seek the Crystal of Harmony?" it asked, the sound reverberating around him.

"It's me, Ryu!" he shouted, standing firm. "I'm here to retrieve it for my crew!"

"Many have come before you, seeking power and glory. What makes you different, Ryu?" the voice questioned, challenging him.

"I fight for my friends, for those who can't fight for themselves!" Ryu declared, determination flooding his veins. "I won't back down until I find them!"

A moment of silence followed before the voice spoke again. "Very well. Prove your worth, but be warned: the echoes can deceive. Trust your heart, and only then may you take the crystal."

As Ryu stepped closer, the whispers intensified, swirling around him like a tempest. Memories flooded his mind—flickers of laughter, pain, and challenges he'd faced alongside his crew. He could hear Kaida's voice encouraging him, Zeno's laughter, and Luna's unwavering support.

"Stay focused!" he shouted against the cacophony. "I won't lose myself to this!"

With every step, the whispers grew louder, urging him to doubt himself. "You're weak. You can't save them. You've always been alone."

"No!" Ryu roared, shaking his head. "I am not alone! I have my friends, my crew, and I will fight for them!"

The voices began to quiet as Ryu pressed forward, determination lighting his path. Finally, he reached the pedestal holding the Crystal of Harmony. He extended his hand, and the crystal pulsed with energy, responding to his presence.

"Take it, Ryu," the voice instructed, softer now. "But remember, the journey ahead will be fraught with danger. Keep your heart true."

With a deep breath, Ryu grasped the crystal, feeling a surge of power course through him. The echoes of the past faded, replaced by clarity and resolve. He could feel the connection to his crew strengthening.

As he turned to leave, the temple shook violently, and the whispers turned to screams. "The trial is not over!" the voice warned. "You must escape before the echoes consume you!"

Ryu raced back through the temple, dodging falling stones and collapsing walls. With the crystal in hand, he felt a renewed strength, propelling him forward. He burst out of the temple just as it crumbled behind him, the echoes fading into silence.

Breathless, Ryu stood on the shore, the crystal glowing brightly in his palm. "I did it," he whispered, a smile breaking across his face. "Now to find my crew."

He knew the path ahead would be challenging, but with the Crystal of Harmony, he felt a renewed sense of purpose. Ryu set off down the beach, determined to reunite with his friends and face whatever lay ahead together.

Kaida blinked as she came to, the bright sun overhead casting warm rays on her face. The sandy beach stretched out before her, but this wasn't the island she remembered. The air was filled with laughter and the sound of waves, but it had an odd, enchanting quality that made her uneasy.

"What is this place?" Kaida murmured, sitting up and brushing the sand off her arms. As she looked around, she noticed the vibrant colors of the landscape: palm trees with colorful blossoms, crystal-clear waters, and, most notably, a group of handsome young men lounging nearby, all dressed in flashy outfits that highlighted their chiseled physiques.

"Welcome to Sexy Boys Island!" one of the young men called out, flashing a dazzling smile. His hair was perfectly styled, and he exuded a charm that was almost overwhelming. "We're here to make your stay unforgettable!"

Kaida narrowed her eyes, suspicious. "Where are my friends? What have you done with them?"

"Your friends?" he echoed, feigning surprise. "Oh, they're around somewhere. But right now, you're the star of the show!" He gestured grandly to the others, who cheered and clapped enthusiastically.

"I'm not interested in being anyone's star!" Kaida shot back, rising to her feet. "I need to find my crew!"

"Now, now, there's no rush," another young man chimed in, his voice smooth as silk. "Why not enjoy our hospitality first? We have games, food, and the most breathtaking views you can imagine!"

Kaida crossed her arms, glaring at them. "I don't want your hospitality! I want to know where my friends are, and I'm not leaving until I find them!"

The first man stepped closer, his expression shifting from playful to serious. "You really don't understand, do you? Once you're here, it's hard to leave. We have a way of making sure our guests... stay happy." He winked, and the group erupted in laughter.

Kaida felt a shiver run down her spine. "What do you mean by that?" she demanded.

"Nothing to worry about, lovely," he replied, leaning in closer. "Just know that you're in for a good time. Let's start with a little game, shall we? It'll help you relax."

"I'm not playing any games!" Kaida snapped, her voice rising. "I need to get back to my crew! They could be in danger!"

"Danger? Here?" one of the boys laughed, shaking his head. "You've got nothing to worry about on Sexy Boys Island. We take care of our own."

"Right," Kaida said, sarcasm dripping from her words. "By keeping them locked away, I suppose?"

At that, the young man's expression darkened slightly. "We don't lock anyone away. But if they want to leave, they have to play by our rules."

Kaida's heart raced. "What kind of rules?"

"Simple! You must win a series of challenges," he said, grinning again. "If you can impress us, we might consider letting you go—along with your friends. But if you fail..." He let the words hang in the air, a smirk playing on his lips.

Kaida squared her shoulders, resolve flooding her. "I'll take your challenges. I won't back down."

"Good choice!" he said, clapping his hands together. "The first challenge is a test of charm and wit. You'll need to impress our audience with your skills. Ready?"

"Let's do this," Kaida replied, determination blazing in her eyes.

As she stepped into the designated area, the crowd gathered around, their eyes sparkling with anticipation. Kaida took a deep breath, recalling the energy of her crew, their laughter, and the bond they shared. She wouldn't let them down.

"Welcome, everyone, to the first challenge!" the man announced dramatically. "Let's see what our new guest has to offer!"

Kaida focused on the audience, her heart racing, but she wouldn't let fear control her. "I may not know what kind of games you play, but I can show you what I'm made of," she declared, her voice steady. "I've fought against formidable foes, and I've never backed down from a challenge."

The crowd murmured, intrigued by her confidence. "Impressive," one of the boys shouted, clearly enjoying the show. "But can you really keep up with us?"

"I've survived worse than this island," Kaida replied, locking eyes with the first young man. "I'll take on your challenges, and I'll win."

"Then let's get started!" he said, grinning as the crowd erupted in cheers. "First up: a dance-off! Show us what you've got!"

Kaida felt a spark of excitement. Dancing wasn't her forte, but she'd faced tougher battles. "Alright, let's dance!" she declared, stepping into the center as music began to play. She focused on the rhythm, channeling her energy and the spirit of her crew, moving with determination.

As she danced, Kaida felt the initial tension ease, her movements flowing with confidence. She twisted and turned, incorporating fierce martial arts moves into her routine. The audience watched in awe, and for a moment, she could feel their skepticism fading.

"Go, Kaida!" a voice shouted from the crowd, igniting a fire within her.

She finished her routine with a powerful kick, striking a pose that left the audience stunned. The applause was thunderous, and the young men exchanged impressed glances.

"Not bad!" the first young man said, a hint of admiration in his voice. "You've got some moves. But the next challenge will be even tougher. Let's see if you can handle it!"

Kaida smiled, her confidence surging. "Bring it on. I'm ready for whatever you throw at me."

With a mischievous grin, he continued, "Next, we'll test your strength! It's a tug-of-war against our strongest contender. Can you hold your ground?"

Kaida nodded, her resolve solidifying. "I won't let you down."

As she prepared for the next challenge, she couldn't shake the feeling that finding her crew was just as important as proving herself here. Whatever it took, she would get back to them and show them that she was more than capable of facing any obstacle, even on an island filled with distractions. The challenges were just the beginning; she had to remain focused on the ultimate goal—reuniting with Ryu, Zeno, and the rest of her friends.

Zeno groaned as he regained consciousness, the sound of crashing waves filling his ears. He sat up, blinking against the bright sun. "Not again," he muttered, pushing himself to his feet. The beach stretched out before him, but it felt eerily different from where he last remembered being.

"Where am I now?" he asked aloud, looking around. The landscape was lush and tropical, with palm trees swaying gently in the breeze. In the distance, he could see towering cliffs and vibrant flowers, but something about the atmosphere felt off.

As he wandered down the shore, Zeno noticed a group of people gathered around a large bonfire, laughing and dancing. They were dressed in bright, colorful outfits, their movements lively and carefree. He approached cautiously, curiosity piquing.

"Hey there, stranger!" one of the dancers called out, a playful grin spreading across his face. "Welcome to the Island of Revelry! Join us for some fun!"

Zeno crossed his arms, skepticism creeping in. "Revelry? Is that what this place is all about? Where are my friends?"

"Friends?" another islander chimed in, his eyes sparkling with mischief. "You mean those who got swept away? Don't worry about them! Here, you'll find all the excitement you need!"

"I'm not here for excitement," Zeno replied firmly, his eyes narrowing. "I need to find my crew. They could be in danger!"

"Danger? Here? Come on!" the first dancer laughed, spinning around dramatically. "This island is all about freedom and fun! Why would you want to leave?"

"Because I don't belong here!" Zeno snapped. "I'm a part of a crew, and I won't stop until I reunite with them."

The dancers exchanged glances, amusement mixed with confusion. "Alright, tough guy," one of them said, stepping closer. "If you're really that determined, you'll have to prove it. We can't just let you waltz in and leave without a challenge."

"What kind of challenge?" Zeno asked, his curiosity piqued despite himself.

"First, we need to see if you can keep up with us," the dancer replied, his tone turning serious. "We're about to have a dance-off. If you can impress us, we might just give you some information about your friends."

"Fine," Zeno said, straightening up. "I'll show you what I can do."

With that, the music began to play—a lively beat that echoed through the island. Zeno felt the rhythm pulse in his veins, and before he knew it, he was moving, his body responding instinctively to the music. He incorporated his swordplay into the dance, blending powerful strikes with fluid movements.

The crowd watched, captivated by his performance. "Not bad for a guy who says he's not here for fun!" one of the islanders called out, cheering him on.

Zeno focused, his energy surging as he executed a series of spins and leaps, using the momentum to add flair to his moves. "I'm not just here to dance! I'm here to find my friends!" he shouted, channeling his determination into every movement.

As he finished, the crowd erupted in applause, and the dancer who had challenged him stepped forward, eyes wide with admiration. "Okay, okay! You've got skills! But the next challenge will be a test of strength. We have a boulder that needs moving, and we want to see if you can handle it."

"Strength? I can do that," Zeno replied, a grin spreading across his face. "Lead the way."

The group led him to a massive boulder perched at the edge of the beach, its surface rough and imposing. "You'll have to push it down the hill and into the ocean," one islander explained. "It's not just about strength; you'll need strategy too."

Zeno nodded, sizing up the boulder. "Alright, stand back," he said, planting his feet firmly on the ground. He took a deep breath, channeling his energy into his core. "Here goes nothing!"

With a powerful grunt, Zeno pushed against the boulder. It didn't budge at first, but he gritted his teeth, applying all his strength. Slowly, the boulder began to roll, picking up speed as he guided it down the slope. The crowd cheered him on, the energy building as he neared the edge of the beach.

"Come on, Zeno! You can do it!" they shouted.

Just as he reached the final stretch, he stumbled slightly, feeling the weight of the boulder shift. "No! Not now!" he yelled, pushing with all his might.

With one final heave, he sent the boulder crashing into the ocean, the splash soaking the cheering crowd. Zeno fell to his knees, panting but exhilarated.

"Wow, you really did it!" one of the islanders exclaimed, eyes wide with respect. "Not many can push that thing!"

"Now tell me what you know about my friends!" Zeno demanded, catching his breath.

The dancer nodded, still impressed. "Alright, alright! We saw them get taken away by the guards in bubbles. They were headed to a different island—an island rumored to be the headquarters of the Executioners!"

Zeno's heart raced. "The Executioners? Where is this island?"

The dancer grinned. "If you want to reach it, you'll need to sail through the treacherous waters. But first, you'll need a ship, and we might know where to find one. Just prove yourself a bit more, and you'll earn our help."

Zeno clenched his fists, resolve hardening within him. "I'll do whatever it takes. I'm not leaving my crew behind, not now, not ever."

"Then let's see what you've got!" the dancer said, excitement twinkling in his eyes. "Welcome to the next challenge!"

Zeno couldn't shake the feeling that time was running out. Every challenge brought him closer to his crew, and he was determined to find them, no matter what trials lay ahead. With renewed vigor, he prepared himself for whatever awaited him on this unpredictable island.

Ryu stood in the center of a large, vibrant arena, the cheers of the crowd echoing off the walls of the island's amphitheater. Colorful banners waved overhead, and the atmosphere buzzed with excitement. This tournament was not just a display of strength; it was his chance to prove himself and gain the respect of the island's inhabitants.

"Welcome, fighters, to the Grand Tournament of Ascendance!" a booming voice announced from the elevated platform. The emcee, a flamboyant man clad in bright armor, gestured dramatically. "Today, we witness the clash of heroes and legends! Our champion will earn glory, fame, and a ship to sail the seas!"

Ryu clenched his fists, determination surging through him. "I need that ship. I won't let my crew down," he muttered under his breath, focusing on the fighters surrounding him. Each one looked formidable, but he wouldn't back down.

The first opponent stepped forward, a tall man with rippling muscles and a fierce glare. "You think you can take me down? I've crushed tougher opponents than you!"

Ryu met his gaze with unwavering confidence. "I'm not here to make friends. I'm here to win."

With a loud bell signaling the start, the two fighters rushed at each other. Ryu ducked low, dodging a powerful punch aimed at his head. He retaliated with a swift kick to the man's midsection, sending him stumbling back. The crowd roared, their cheers fueling Ryu's adrenaline.

"You're quick, I'll give you that!" the man shouted, regaining his balance. "But let's see how you handle this!" He charged forward, unleashing a flurry of punches.

Ryu dodged and weaved, focusing on his opponent's movements. "I've faced tougher than you," he said, gritting his teeth as he caught one of the punches, twisting it to his advantage. He slammed his elbow into the man's jaw, sending him sprawling to the ground.

The audience erupted in applause. "Ryu! Ryu! Ryu!" they chanted, their energy electrifying the arena. Ryu felt a surge of pride; this was his moment.

The emcee grinned from his perch. "What an impressive display! Our challenger has taken down the first fighter! Who will step up next?"

A petite girl with fiery red hair and a fierce look in her eyes strode into the arena. "I'll take you on," she declared, confidence radiating from her. "Don't underestimate me!"

"Bring it on," Ryu replied, grinning. "I won't go easy on you just because you're smaller."

"Good! I wouldn't want you to," she shot back, her smile unwavering.

As the bell rang again, they circled each other, assessing their strengths. Ryu made the first move, launching himself forward with a high kick. The girl ducked under it, rolling to the side and springing up, launching a rapid series of punches.

Ryu blocked and countered, his instincts guiding him. "You're fast! But can you keep up?" he challenged, dodging another of her swift strikes.

"I can do more than keep up!" she exclaimed, unleashing a powerful kick that connected with Ryu's side. He staggered but quickly regained his footing.

"Impressive! But I'm not out yet!" Ryu grinned, channeling his energy into a spinning backfist that caught her off guard. She tumbled back but rolled smoothly, regaining her stance.

The crowd was on the edge of their seats, chanting their encouragement. "Fight! Fight! Fight!"

With renewed determination, Ryu pressed forward, using a combination of punches and agile movements to keep her on her toes. "You're good!" he called out, admiration shining in his eyes. "What's your name?"

"Lira!" she shouted, dodging another of his strikes. "And you're not half bad yourself, Ryu!"

Finally, with a burst of energy, Ryu performed a high leap, bringing down a powerful elbow strike that landed right beside Lira, causing a shockwave that knocked her off balance. She fell to the ground, panting but laughing.

"You're stronger than I thought," she admitted, pushing herself up. "But I'm not done yet!"

Ryu extended a hand to help her up. "You put up a great fight. I respect that."

As she took his hand, the emcee stepped in, raising his arms to silence the crowd. "What an incredible match! Both fighters showed remarkable skill and heart! But our champion today is Ryu!"

Cheers erupted once more, and Ryu felt a swell of pride. As he caught his breath, Lira approached him, a serious expression replacing her earlier playfulness.

"Ryu, you fought well," she said, her tone shifting. "But I can see you're not just here for glory. You're searching for something more."

"Yeah," he replied, feeling the weight of his mission. "I need to find my crew. They're scattered across different islands, and time is running out."

Lira nodded, her eyes narrowing thoughtfully. "If you're looking for a ship, I might be able to help. I have a small vessel that could get you where you need to go, but first, I need to know you can be trusted."

"I promise, I'll do whatever it takes to get my crew back," Ryu vowed, sincerity in his voice. "What do you need me to do?"

"There's a group of thugs on the island who've been causing trouble. If you can help me deal with them, I'll give you the ship," Lira explained, her gaze steady. "It's a small price for my trust."

Ryu nodded, his determination igniting. "Consider it done. I'll take care of those thugs."

"Good," she said, a smile returning to her lips. "Meet me by the docks in an hour, and we'll get you set up. Just remember, this island values strength and loyalty. Show them what you've got."

"I will," Ryu promised, feeling the weight of responsibility lift slightly. With Lira's help, he would get back to his crew and take on whatever challenges lay ahead. He turned to face the cheering crowd, adrenaline still coursing through him.

"Now, let's see what this island has to offer," he said to himself, ready to prove that he was more than just a fighter—he was a leader, and he would stop at nothing to reunite with his friends.

Ryu stood at the docks, the salty sea breeze whipping through his hair as he waited for Lira. He felt a surge of anticipation, fueled by the knowledge that he was one step closer to reuniting with his crew. As he scanned the shoreline, a familiar figure caught his eye—a silhouette stumbling along the beach, looking lost and disoriented.

"Is that...?" Ryu squinted, his heart racing as he recognized the outline. "Theo!"

Without a second thought, he sprinted down the dock and across the sandy beach, calling out, "Theo! Over here!"

Theo turned at the sound of his name, his eyes widening in disbelief. "Ryu? Is that really you?" He rushed toward Ryu, and they met in a bone-crushing hug.

"I thought I'd never find you!" Ryu exclaimed, pulling back to look at his friend's face. "What happened? Are you alright?"

"I'm fine! Just a little lost, you know?" Theo laughed, though Ryu could see the tension in his eyes. "After we got separated, I woke up on another island. I was trying to track down our crew, but it's been chaos everywhere. I didn't know where to go."

"Same here," Ryu said, relief flooding through him. "But I've been fighting in a tournament to prove my worth and earn a ship to find everyone."

"A tournament? That sounds intense!" Theo replied, his eyes sparkling with excitement. "Did you win?"

"Yeah, but there's more to it," Ryu said, lowering his voice. "I need to help Lira deal with some troublemakers on this island before I can get us a ship. Have you seen anyone else? Kaida? Zeno?"

"No, I haven't seen them since the bubble incident," Theo replied, a frown crossing his face. "I was hoping you would have a lead on them."

Ryu shook his head, frustration bubbling beneath the surface. "I'll find them, I promise. But first, let's focus on this threat Lira mentioned. If we can clear that out, we can get the ship and start searching for the others."

"Alright, let's do it!" Theo said, determination igniting in his eyes. "What's the plan?"

"Lira said there are a group of thugs causing trouble near the eastern edge of the island. If we can take them out, we'll gain Lira's trust and get the ship," Ryu explained, already feeling the adrenaline of the upcoming fight.

Theo nodded, his expression serious. "Lead the way. I've been itching for a fight since I got here!"

They made their way toward the eastern edge, navigating through dense foliage and vibrant flowers. Ryu felt a sense of camaraderie building between them, their bond stronger than ever after everything they had been through.

"So, how's your training been?" Ryu asked, trying to lighten the mood. "Still practicing those crazy inventions?"

"Of course!" Theo laughed, scratching the back of his head. "I've been working on some new gadgets, but I need to test them out in real combat. Just haven't had the chance yet."

"Maybe you can use them against these thugs," Ryu suggested, a grin spreading across his face. "I can't wait to see what you've come up with."

As they approached the edge of the forest, the sounds of raucous laughter and shouting reached their ears. Ryu exchanged a glance with Theo, both of them understanding the seriousness of their mission.

"Ready?" Ryu asked, his voice low and steady.

"Always," Theo replied, pulling out a small device from his pocket—a compact grappling hook. "Let's show them what we've got."

They crept closer, peering through the trees to see a group of rough-looking thugs gathered around a campfire, their weapons glinting in the sunlight. The thugs seemed to be celebrating, completely unaware of the two newcomers watching them.

"Looks like we caught them at a good time," Ryu whispered, eyeing the largest thug, who was boasting loudly about his latest con. "We need to take them out before they realize we're here."

"Leave it to me," Theo said, gripping his grappling hook. "I'll swing in and create a distraction. You follow up with an attack."

"Got it," Ryu nodded, adrenaline pumping through him. "On three."

They counted down together. "One... two... three!"

Theo launched himself from the trees, using the grappling hook to swing into the camp, landing gracefully on his feet. "Hey, losers! Having a party without me?" he shouted, a smirk on his face.

The thugs turned, surprise flooding their expressions. "What the—who are you?" the leader growled, reaching for his weapon.

Ryu seized the moment, charging in with a fierce battle cry. "Now!"

He tackled the nearest thug, sending him sprawling to the ground. Theo was right behind him, using a series of gadgets to disable weapons and create chaos in the camp.

"Nice distraction!" Ryu called out, landing a powerful kick on another thug. "Keep it up!"

Theo grinned as he deployed a smoke bomb, filling the air with a thick fog. "They won't see what hit them!"

The thugs scrambled, trying to find their footing in the chaos. Ryu could feel the excitement of battle coursing through him as he exchanged blows with the criminals.

"Together!" Ryu shouted, coordinating their movements. They worked seamlessly, Ryu's martial prowess complementing Theo's quick thinking and clever gadgets.

After a fierce fight, the last thug collapsed, groaning on the ground. Ryu and Theo stood over them, panting but victorious.

"Not bad for a day's work," Ryu said, catching his breath. "Now let's find Lira and get that ship."

Theo nodded, a triumphant grin on his face. "I'm ready to get out of here and find the rest of the crew. Let's go!"

As they made their way back toward the docks, Ryu felt a renewed sense of purpose. Together, they would find their friends and take on whatever challenges awaited them. No matter how far they were apart, their bond would guide them back to one another.

As Ryu and Theo approached the camp, the air crackled with tension. The remnants of the thugs they had just defeated scattered in the background, but Lira's troublemakers were a different breed—more organized, and clearly ready for a fight.

Ryu glanced at Theo, determination in his eyes. "These guys look tougher than the last batch. Are you ready?"

"Always," Theo replied, adjusting his grip on the grappling hook. "Let's make this quick. I've got some surprises up my sleeve."

The duo crept closer, hidden behind the dense foliage. They could see Lira's troublemakers—roughly six of them, armed and boasting as they counted their ill-gotten gains around a makeshift table.

"Think they can just take our turf?" one of the troublemakers sneered, slamming a fist on the table. "They'll regret ever stepping foot on this island!"

"Let them come! We'll show them what real power looks like," another thug replied, brandishing a knife with a menacing grin.

Ryu exchanged a glance with Theo, their plan solidifying. "On three, we charge in," he whispered. "One... two... three!"

With a shout, Ryu and Theo burst from their hiding place, launching themselves into the fray.

"Hey, losers! We're here to clean up this mess!" Ryu yelled, charging at the nearest thug, who barely had time to react before Ryu delivered a powerful punch that sent him reeling.

Theo, meanwhile, swung his grappling hook, snagging another thug and pulling him off balance. "You picked the wrong fight!" he shouted, using the distraction to deliver a swift kick to the thug's stomach.

The troublemakers quickly regrouped, their confidence shaken but not broken. "Get them!" the leader barked, pointing his knife at Ryu. "Don't let them get away!"

Ryu grinned, dodging a swing from the leader. "Is that all you've got?" he taunted, flipping backward to avoid a knife aimed at him.

"Show him, Ryu!" Theo shouted, launching a smoke bomb into the center of the group. The fog filled the air, and chaos erupted as the troublemakers struggled to find their targets.

Ryu took advantage of the confusion, his fists flying as he landed a few quick strikes. "Theo! We need to separate them!" he yelled through the thick smoke.

"On it!" Theo responded, deploying a series of flash grenades that burst brightly, temporarily blinding the thugs. "Let's split them up!"

"Nice move!" Ryu called, taking out another thug with a well-placed kick. "Just keep them busy while I take down the leader!"

In the chaos, the leader swung wildly, trying to find Ryu in the smoke. "Where are you, coward?" he growled, clearly agitated.

"Right here!" Ryu replied, emerging from the smoke with a fierce punch aimed directly at the leader's jaw. The impact echoed, but the leader staggered rather than falling.

"You think you can take me down that easily?" the thug hissed, wiping blood from his mouth. "You've got another thing coming!"

"I've faced worse than you!" Ryu shot back, his resolve hardening. He could feel the adrenaline pumping through his veins, heightening his senses.

Meanwhile, Theo was engaged with two other troublemakers, using his gadgets to create diversions and confuse them. "You guys are outclassed!" he called out, dodging a wild swing from one thug. "Just give up!"

One of the troublemakers growled, clearly agitated. "Shut up! We'll take you both down!" He lunged at Theo, who expertly sidestepped, sending the thug crashing into his partner.

"Nice teamwork!" Ryu shouted, seeing Theo's maneuver. "Let's finish this!"

Ryu focused on the leader again, who was now breathing heavily. "You're tougher than you look," Ryu admitted, preparing for another strike. "But I won't hold back anymore!"

With renewed determination, Ryu charged forward, fists raised, while Theo launched a small explosive device that exploded near the thugs, creating a blinding flash and smoke. The troublemakers, disoriented, stumbled back.

Ryu seized the moment. "Now, Theo!"

Together, they moved in sync, Ryu aiming for the leader while Theo kept the other thugs occupied. The fight became a whirlwind of fists, kicks, and quick movements, each moment filled with tension as neither side was willing to back down.

"Don't underestimate us!" the leader spat, trying to regain his footing. "We're not just a bunch of thugs!"

"Then show me what you've got!" Ryu challenged, launching forward for another strike.

In the midst of the chaos, Theo shouted, "We're not going to let you run this island anymore!"

The struggle continued, each punch and kick resonating with the weight of their determination. The clash of wills filled the air, and the outcome hung in the balance, with no clear victor emerging yet from the storm of fists and fury.

As the smoke began to clear, Ryu and Theo stood over the defeated troublemakers, panting but victorious. The thugs groaned on the ground, their bravado stripped away. Ryu wiped sweat from his brow, turning to Theo with a grin.

"Did you see that last move? I think I finally perfected my uppercut!" Ryu exclaimed, chuckling.

Theo laughed, shaking his head. "You mean the one where you nearly knocked yourself out? But yeah, that was pretty impressive! We make a good team."

Just then, a familiar voice rang out from behind them. "You two sure know how to make an entrance." Lira stepped forward, her expression a mixture of relief and admiration. "I heard the commotion from a distance. I wasn't sure what to expect."

Ryu straightened, a triumphant smile spreading across his face. "We took care of those troublemakers for you. They won't be causing any more chaos on your island."

Lira surveyed the defeated thugs, her eyes narrowing. "You really did a number on them. I'm impressed. With their absence, we can finally restore some peace around here."

Theo nodded, his enthusiasm bubbling over. "Now about that ship you promised us. We're ready to find our friend Kaida!"

"Right," Lira said, her expression turning serious. "Follow me; the ship is docked a little further down the coast."

As they made their way to the docks, Ryu and Theo couldn't help but feel a sense of excitement. They were finally one step closer to reuniting with their crew.

"So, what's the plan once we find Kaida?" Theo asked, glancing at Ryu.

"We need to find out what happened to her and the others," Ryu replied, his voice firm. "We can't let the Executioners get away with this."

Lira led them to a small but sturdy ship, its sails billowing gently in the breeze. "This is your vessel. She's fast and reliable, perfect for navigating the seas."

Ryu's eyes lit up at the sight. "This is perfect! Thank you, Lira."

"You've earned it," she said, giving them both a warm smile. "Just be careful out there. The waters are treacherous, and the Executioners have eyes everywhere."

Theo jumped onto the ship's deck, checking the rigging and supplies. "We're going to need all the supplies we can get. I'll make sure everything is in order before we leave."

Ryu joined him, scanning the ship. "Let's make sure we're ready for anything. We don't know what kind of trouble we might run into."

As they worked, Lira watched them, her expression thoughtful. "You two have a strong bond. It's inspiring to see. I know you'll do whatever it takes to find your friend."

"Absolutely," Ryu replied, determination etched in his features. "We won't stop until we find Kaida and the rest of our crew."

After a few minutes of preparing the ship, Theo turned to Ryu, a mischievous glint in his eye. "Think we can make it a race to see who can tie the best knot?"

Ryu raised an eyebrow, smirking. "You're on! But don't be too upset when I win."

"Dream on!" Theo laughed, and they both dove into the task with renewed energy, the tension of the previous fight fading as camaraderie took its place.

Once everything was in order, Lira approached them one last time. "Before you set off, take this." She handed Ryu a small, ornate compass. "It will help you navigate to the island where I last heard of the Executioners. Be careful, and remember: trust each other and stay strong."

Ryu took the compass, his heart swelling with gratitude. "Thank you, Lira. We'll be careful. And we'll come back to visit once we've got Kaida and the crew safe."

"Good luck," Lira said, stepping back as they climbed aboard the ship. "I'll be watching from here. You've got this."

With a final wave, Ryu and Theo set sail, the wind filling the sails and propelling them forward. Ryu stood at the bow, gripping the compass tightly.

"Alright, Theo! Let's head to the last known location of the Executioners!" Ryu shouted over the roar of the waves.

"On it!" Theo replied, adjusting the sails to catch the wind just right. "With this ship, we'll be there in no time!"

As they sailed away from the island, Ryu couldn't shake the feeling of anticipation. They were on a mission to find their friend, and nothing would stop them. The ocean stretched out before them, full of possibilities and dangers, but together, they were ready to face whatever awaited them.

"Let's find Kaida!" Ryu declared, determination shining in his eyes.

"Yeah! And whoever stands in our way better watch out!" Theo added, a grin spreading across his face.

With their spirits high and their friendship stronger than ever, they ventured into the unknown, ready to reclaim their crew and take on the world.

As Ryu and Theo sailed through the churning waves, the sun dipped lower in the sky, casting a warm golden hue over the ocean. The ship sliced through the water with purpose, its sails billowing in the brisk wind. Ryu stood at the bow, his eyes scanning the horizon, the compass clutched tightly in his hand.

"Do you think we're getting close?" Ryu asked, turning back to Theo, who was adjusting the ship's course.

"We should be," Theo replied, glancing at the compass. "According to Lira, the Executioners' hideout is on an island not too far from here. We just need to keep an eye out for any signs."

Ryu nodded, a mix of excitement and anxiety bubbling within him. "I just wish we had more information about what we're walking into. If the Executioners are there, they'll be ready for us."

Theo adjusted the sails, his brow furrowing. "True, but we have the element of surprise. They won't expect us to show up this soon."

"Right. We need to be smart about this," Ryu said, pacing the deck. "Once we land, we'll have to gather intel before charging in. I want to know what kind of defenses they have in place."

Theo leaned against the ship's railing, crossing his arms. "Good thinking. Maybe we can find some locals who know the area. If anyone can help us, it'll be them."

Just then, the sharp cry of a seagull echoed overhead, pulling Ryu's attention back to the sea. "Look!" he exclaimed, pointing toward a distant speck on the horizon. "Is that the island?"

Theo squinted into the sunlight. "Could be! Let's get closer and check it out."

As they drew nearer, the outline of the island became clearer. Towering cliffs rose majestically from the water, and a thick forest blanketed the land. Ryu felt a rush of determination.

"Alright, let's find a place to dock," he instructed, his voice steady. "We need to be careful; we don't want to give away our presence too soon."

Theo maneuvered the ship expertly, navigating through the rocky waters until they found a secluded cove. Once anchored, they prepared to disembark, gathering their supplies and weapons.

"Ready?" Ryu asked, glancing at Theo.

"Always," Theo replied, adjusting his grappling hook. "Let's do this."

They stepped off the ship, the warm sand beneath their feet contrasting with the cool ocean breeze. The sounds of the forest surrounded them—birds chirping, leaves rustling. Ryu took a deep breath, steeling himself for whatever lay ahead.

"Stay low," Ryu whispered, leading the way into the dense trees. They moved cautiously, keeping their voices low as they approached the edge of the forest, where they could get a better view of the island.

"Look!" Theo pointed toward a clearing where a small village lay nestled between the trees. "There might be someone there who can help us."

As they crept closer, Ryu noticed a group of people gathered in the village square. They seemed tense, whispering amongst themselves, casting furtive glances toward a larger building at the center.

"Something's not right," Ryu muttered, his instincts kicking in. "Let's observe for a moment."

Theo nodded, and they crouched behind a large tree, watching the villagers. Ryu could see fear etched on their faces. He turned to Theo, concern shadowing his features.

"Do you think the Executioners have been here?"

"Could be," Theo said, his voice barely above a whisper. "They might be intimidating the locals, trying to keep them quiet about what they're doing. We need to find out more."

Suddenly, a loud voice boomed from the building. "You will obey! Or face the consequences!" A tall figure emerged, flanked by a couple of armed guards, their expressions menacing. The villagers cowered, and Ryu's heart raced.

"That's definitely an Executioner," Ryu said, clenching his fists. "They're using fear to control this place."

"Then we need to act," Theo replied, determination flickering in his eyes. "But we can't just rush in. We need a plan."

Ryu nodded, watching as the guards enforced the figure's commands. "We should try to get some information before we make our move. Maybe one of the villagers can tell us what's going on."

"Good idea," Theo agreed. "Let's look for someone who seems less frightened."

They began to move through the trees, keeping their eyes peeled for a villager who might be willing to talk. As they slipped deeper into the shadows, Ryu felt a sense of urgency gnawing at him.

"Kaida could be in trouble," Ryu murmured, his thoughts racing. "We can't let her down."

"I know," Theo replied, his tone reassuring. "But rushing in without a plan won't help her either. We'll find a way to get her back."

They continued to search for a villager who might provide answers, determined to gather intel before making their next move. Every moment felt critical, the weight of their mission pressing heavily on their shoulders.

Finally, Ryu spotted a woman sitting alone on a weathered log, her eyes downcast. "Over there," he whispered to Theo, nodding toward her. "She looks like she might be willing to talk."

As they approached, the woman looked up, her gaze filled with fear. "Please, don't hurt me," she stammered, backing away slightly.

Ryu held up his hands. "No, we're not here to hurt you. We want to help. We're looking for someone named Kaida. Have you seen her?"

The woman's eyes widened, and she hesitated, glancing around as if fearing eavesdroppers. "Kaida... She's been taken by the Executioners. They... they've brought her to their headquarters."

"Where is it?" Theo pressed, urgency coloring his voice.

"Through the forest, near the cliffs," she said, her voice trembling. "But you must be careful. They have guards everywhere, and if they catch you... it won't end well."

Ryu felt a fire ignite within him. "We'll take our chances. Thank you for the information."

The woman nodded, relief washing over her face. "Please... save her. She's not like the others. She's brave."

"We will," Ryu promised, exchanging a determined look with Theo. "We're getting Kaida back."

As they turned to leave, Ryu felt a surge of hope. They had a lead now, and with that lead came the possibility of reuniting with their crew. The path ahead would be dangerous, but they were ready to face whatever challenges awaited them. With renewed determination, they headed back into the forest, setting their sights on the Executioners' stronghold.

Kaida was dragged through the vibrant streets of Sexy Boys Island, the laughter and music of the nearby festivities fading into a distant memory. The guards from the Executioners gripped her arms tightly, their faces impassive as they escorted her toward the docks. She struggled against their hold, trying to break free.

"Let me go! You can't do this!" Kaida shouted, her voice filled with defiance. But her words fell on deaf ears as the guards tightened their grip.

"Save your breath," one of the guards sneered. "You'll need it when we hand you over to the boss."

Kaida clenched her teeth, fighting to remain calm. She had to think of a way out of this. Glancing around, she noticed the colorful banners fluttering in the breeze and the distant sounds of laughter. This was her home, and it felt surreal that she was being taken away from it.

"Stop struggling," another guard hissed. "You're only making this harder for yourself."

As they reached the docks, Kaida spotted a ship docked at the end, its dark sails billowing ominously. Panic surged through her. "What do you want with me?" she demanded, her heart racing. "You can't just take me like this!"

"Enough with the questions," the first guard barked, pushing her forward. "Get on the ship."

Kaida took a deep breath, steeling herself. She had to remain strong, for Ryu and Theo. They would come for her. She refused to let fear take over.

Meanwhile, back in the forest, Ryu and Theo were navigating through the dense underbrush, their minds racing with possibilities.

"Did you catch what she said?" Theo asked, glancing back at Ryu. "The Executioners are holding Kaida at their headquarters."

"I did," Ryu replied, determination etching his features. "We need to move quickly. The longer we wait, the more dangerous it gets for her."

"Let's make a plan," Theo suggested as they continued deeper into the forest. "We can't just rush in without knowing how many guards they have or what kind of defenses are in place."

Ryu nodded, the weight of their mission pressing heavily on him. "You're right. We need to be smart about this. Let's find a vantage point where we can observe the headquarters before making any moves."

They soon stumbled upon a hill that overlooked the Executioners' stronghold, a dark fortress built into the cliffs. Ryu's heart sank at the sight. The area was heavily guarded, with sentries patrolling the perimeter and watchtowers looming above.

"Look at all those guards," Theo whispered, his eyes widening. "How are we supposed to get in there?"

"We'll need a distraction," Ryu mused, his mind racing. "If we can draw some of them away, it'll give us a better chance to slip in unnoticed."

"Do you have anything in mind?" Theo asked, scanning the area.

"I think I might," Ryu replied, a spark of inspiration igniting within him. "If we create a noise on the opposite side of the fortress, we can lure some of the guards away. We could use that opportunity to sneak around and find Kaida."

Theo nodded, excitement flickering in his eyes. "That could work. But we need to be careful. If we're caught, it'll be game over for us."

"We won't get caught," Ryu said confidently. "We're going to do this together. We've come too far to back down now."

As they strategized, Kaida found herself aboard the ship, the crew of the Executioners eyeing her with disdain. She stood defiantly, her chin held high despite the fear gnawing at her insides.

"Welcome aboard, Kaida," a tall, imposing figure said, stepping forward. "I'm Goran, and you're going to wish you'd behaved yourself."

"Goran..." Kaida muttered, recognizing the name from the stories whispered among the islanders. "You won't get away with this."

He chuckled, a sinister smile spreading across his face. "Oh, but I already have. Your friends are out there somewhere, scrambling to find you. It's only a matter of time before they come crashing into our trap."

Kaida's heart sank at the realization. "They won't stop until they find me."

"Exactly," Goran replied, his tone dripping with malice. "And when they do, it'll make for quite the show. I can't wait to see how it all unfolds."

Meanwhile, Ryu and Theo were preparing their distraction, gathering rocks and branches to create a noise far from the fortress.

"Are you ready?" Ryu asked, glancing at Theo, who was tying a bundle of branches together.

"Just about," Theo said, a determined glint in his eyes. "Once we set this up, we'll need to act fast."

"Let's do it," Ryu replied, a fire igniting within him. "For Kaida!"

With that, they set their plan into motion, the tension in the air palpable as they maneuvered through the trees, each step bringing them closer to their goal. They knew that every second counted, and the fate of their friend rested in their hands.

As Ryu and Theo set their plan in motion, they moved stealthily through the underbrush, their hearts pounding in unison. The Executioners' fortress loomed ahead, an imposing structure of dark stone that seemed to absorb the sunlight. Ryu felt a mix of determination and trepidation as they approached the edge of the clearing.

"Okay, we need to get this distraction going," Ryu whispered, glancing at Theo. "Where do you think we should place it?"

Theo scanned the area, his brow furrowed in concentration. "What about over there?" He pointed to a cluster of rocks just beyond the tree line, a few dozen yards away from the nearest guard tower. "If we throw something heavy, it should create a loud enough noise to draw them away."

Ryu nodded. "Let's do it. I'll throw the first rock. You keep an eye on the guards and let me know when to go."

"Got it," Theo replied, crouching low as Ryu picked up a sizable stone, feeling the weight in his hands. He steadied himself, taking a deep breath to calm his racing heart.

"Here goes nothing," he murmured, launching the rock toward the cluster. It landed with a resounding thud, sending up a spray of dirt and gravel.

"Now!" Theo hissed, and they both crouched low, watching as several guards turned their heads, eyes narrowing at the source of the noise.

"What was that?" one guard shouted, pointing toward the disturbance. "Go check it out!"

As the guards began to move, Ryu felt a rush of adrenaline. "Let's go!" he urged, darting forward with Theo close behind.

They slipped past the remaining guards, moving quickly but quietly, adrenaline fueling their every step. As they neared the fortress, the sounds of the guards calling to one another faded behind them, replaced by the rustling of leaves and the distant sound of crashing waves.

"Over here," Theo whispered, gesturing toward a side entrance that was partially concealed by overgrown vines. Ryu nodded, and they slipped inside, the air cooler and darker than outside.

Inside, they found themselves in a narrow hallway lined with dimly lit torches. The stone walls felt cold to the touch, and the atmosphere was thick with tension. Ryu could hear faint voices coming from a nearby room.

"Do you think Kaida's in here?" Ryu asked, peering around the corner.

"Maybe," Theo replied, holding his breath as he leaned in to listen. "We have to be cautious."

Just then, a loud crash echoed through the hall, and the voices grew louder. Ryu's heart raced. "That sounded like a fight. We need to hurry!"

They moved quickly, their footsteps silent on the stone floor. As they approached a heavy wooden door, Ryu could see a flicker of movement through the cracks.

"On three," Ryu whispered, glancing at Theo. "One... two... three!"

With a swift push, they burst through the door, ready for anything. But what they saw took them by surprise.

Kaida stood in the center of the room, facing off against a group of Executioner thugs. She looked fierce, her stance firm as she deflected their attacks, but she was clearly outnumbered.

"Kaida!" Ryu shouted, his voice cutting through the chaos.

Her head snapped around, and a flash of relief crossed her face. "Ryu! Theo! You found me!"

"Hang on!" Theo yelled, rushing to her side. Ryu followed, his heart pounding as he took in the scene.

The Executioners paused for a moment, confusion flickering in their eyes. "What the—?" one of them began, but Ryu wasted no time.

"Let's take them down!" Ryu charged forward, adrenaline surging through him. He landed a solid punch on the nearest thug, sending him sprawling.

"Nice move!" Kaida shouted, quickly sidestepping an attack and countering with a swift kick that sent another guard crashing into the wall.

"I'm glad we made it in time!" Ryu replied, dodging a wild swing from behind. He grabbed the thug's arm, twisting it behind him before throwing him aside.

"We need to clear this room and get out of here!" Theo called, tossing a chair into the fray to create a barrier.

"Right! But where's their main control center?" Kaida asked, her eyes scanning the room for any signs of a way out.

"There's a staircase over there," Ryu pointed, catching his breath for a moment. "If we can get to the top, we might find a way to the exit."

"Let's move!" Theo urged, and they pushed forward, dispatching guards as they fought their way to the staircase. The sound of combat echoed in their ears, fueling their resolve.

As they reached the base of the staircase, Ryu glanced back at Kaida. "Are you okay? Did they hurt you?"

"I'm fine, just a little outnumbered," she replied with a determined grin. "Let's finish this."

With that, they ascended the stairs, moving in unison. The air grew thicker with tension as they climbed, and the sounds of battle began to fade behind them. Ryu could feel his heart racing, not just from the physical exertion but from the fear of what awaited them at the top.

"Here goes nothing," Ryu said, reaching for the door at the top of the stairs. With a deep breath, he flung it open.

What lay before them was a vast room filled with maps, charts, and a large table at the center. But it was the figure standing at the far end, a smirk playing on his lips, that made Ryu's blood run cold.

"Welcome," Goran said, his voice smooth and taunting. "I was wondering when you'd show up."

"Let Kaida go!" Ryu demanded, stepping forward, fists clenched.

Goran chuckled, leaning casually against the table. "And why would I do that? This is just the beginning of our fun."

"We're not here to play games," Kaida shot back, her eyes narrowing. "We'll take you down."

"Oh, I look forward to that," Goran replied, his expression shifting to one of cold menace. "But first, let's see what you're really made of."

With that, the tension in the room snapped, and the battle was on once again. Ryu felt a surge of adrenaline as they charged forward, ready to fight for their friend and take down the Executioners once and for all.

As the tension in the room thickened, Zeno emerged from the shadows, his presence both commanding and ominous. With a swift motion, he raised his sword, the blade shimmering with a faint, otherworldly light.

"Not so fast, Goran," Zeno declared, stepping forward with confidence. "You won't be getting away this time."

Goran's smirk faltered for a moment as he turned to face Zeno, surprise flashing in his eyes. "You think you can intimidate me with a fancy sword trick? How quaint."

Zeno's grip on his sword tightened, a determined glint in his eyes. "You have no idea what I'm capable of. With this sword, I can manipulate the very air around me. Watch closely."

He swung his blade with a fluid motion, and to everyone's astonishment, a wave of energy radiated from the tip, slicing through the air. The energy formed into phantom blades that danced around him, swirling and flickering like fireflies.

"What is this sorcery?" one of the Executioners exclaimed, eyes wide with fear.

"It's not sorcery," Zeno replied, his voice steady. "It's the culmination of my training. You see, my sword isn't just a weapon; it's an extension of my will. I can control it in ways you wouldn't believe."

"Enough of this!" Goran shouted, regaining his composure. "You think tricks will save you? You're just prolonging your inevitable defeat."

"Maybe," Zeno countered, stepping closer, the phantom blades circling him like a protective barrier. "But I'd rather fight than cower. You've taken my friends and harmed those I care about. This ends here."

Ryu glanced at Kaida, their eyes meeting with a shared determination. "We're not backing down, Goran. You're outnumbered, and your time is up."

With a growl, Goran surged forward, but Zeno was ready. "Now, let's see how you handle this!" He unleashed the phantom blades, sending them flying toward Goran like a volley of arrows.

"Watch out!" Kaida shouted, but Goran merely laughed, raising his arms as if to ward them off. The blades sliced through the air, some ricocheting off the walls while others narrowly missed him.

"Pathetic!" he yelled, dodging effortlessly. "You think your tricks will work on me? I'm not some common thug!"

But Zeno didn't falter. "No, you're worse. You're the kind of monster who thinks he can toy with people's lives without consequence."

As Goran continued to dodge, Zeno focused his energy, directing the blades with precision. They swirled around him, converging on Goran from multiple angles, forcing him to move and counter them constantly.

"Enough!" Goran roared, frustration evident in his voice. He charged forward, attempting to close the distance. "You think you can defeat me with some fancy moves?"

Zeno smirked, channeling his focus. "It's not just about the moves. It's about the intent behind them." He shifted his stance, redirecting the phantom blades to converge in a spiral around Goran, tightening their formation.

Caught off guard, Goran stumbled, his momentum disrupted. "What are you doing?!" he yelled, panic seeping into his bravado.

"I'm giving you a taste of your own medicine," Zeno replied coolly. "Let's see how well you handle being outmatched."

With a swift flick of his wrist, Zeno sent the blades crashing toward Goran, who barely managed to evade them, but one blade grazed his arm, leaving a deep cut. He winced, rage boiling within him. "You'll pay for that!"

"Not if we have anything to say about it," Ryu chimed in, launching himself at Goran from the side. He landed a powerful kick that sent Goran staggering backward.

"Watch it!" Goran spat, regaining his footing. He glared at Ryu, but before he could retaliate, Kaida joined the fray, delivering a well-placed punch that sent him reeling again.

"This is for everyone you've hurt!" she shouted, her fists flying.

The Executioners, realizing their leader was struggling, rushed to his aid, but Zeno expertly manipulated the phantom blades to keep them at bay, ensuring they couldn't reach Goran.

"Stay back!" Zeno commanded, his voice ringing with authority. "This is between us."

"Goran, we need backup!" one of the guards yelled, but Goran waved them off, fury burning in his eyes.

"No! I can handle this!" he bellowed, his pride pushing him further into the fight.

As Ryu and Kaida fought alongside Zeno, the tide of battle began to shift. They worked seamlessly together, combining their strengths. Each punch, kick, and swing of Zeno's blade created a rhythm that pushed Goran back, cornering him against the wall.

"This is just the beginning!" Goran shouted, desperation creeping into his voice. "You'll regret this!"

Zeno stepped forward, his sword glowing brighter. "No, Goran. This is where your reign of terror ends."

With that declaration, the three friends pressed their attack, determined to take down the Executioners and rescue their friend. As they closed in on Goran, the atmosphere crackled with energy, and it was clear: the fight for freedom was just beginning.

Just as the intensity of the battle reached its peak, a sudden crackle of energy filled the air. Out of the shadows, Luna appeared, her eyes shimmering with a fierce determination. "Enough of this!" she declared, her voice cutting through the chaos like a bolt of lightning.

The moment she raised her hand, dark clouds began to gather above the fortress, swirling ominously. "You think you can take my friends and get away with it?" she shouted, her voice steady despite the storm brewing around her.

Goran turned, his eyes widening as he recognized the power gathering in Luna's grasp. "What are you doing? You can't—"

"Lightning Bolt!" Luna cried, unleashing a torrent of electric energy that arced toward Goran. The raw power crackled through the air, illuminating the room in a brilliant flash.

"NO!" Goran shouted, his voice filled with both fear and rage as the lightning struck him directly. The force of the blow sent him flying back, crashing into the wall with a thunderous impact.

As the dust settled, a stunned silence fell over the room. Goran lay motionless, the threat finally neutralized.

"Luna!" Ryu exclaimed, rushing over to her side. "You made it!"

"Of course, I did," she replied, a proud smile breaking through her earlier tension. "I wouldn't let you guys fight without me."

"Thanks for showing up just in time," Kaida added, her relief palpable. "We couldn't have done it without you."

Theo looked around the room, breathing a sigh of relief. "Now that Goran's out of the way, we need to regroup and figure out our next move."

Zeno nodded, sheathing his sword. "We've done well, but there may be more Executioners lurking. We can't let our guard down yet."

"Then let's get back to the ship!" Ryu urged, glancing toward the staircase. "Lira's waiting for us, and we have to get out of here before reinforcements arrive."

As they made their way down the stairs, the group moved in unison, adrenaline still coursing through their veins. The echoes of battle faded behind them, replaced by the sound of their hurried footsteps.

Once outside, the sun greeted them, casting a warm light on the battlefield. They sprinted towards the shoreline where Lira's ship, a sleek vessel with shimmering sails, bobbed gently on the waves.

"Is that her ship?" Theo asked, pointing excitedly.

"Looks like it," Ryu replied, his spirits lifting as they approached. "Lira really came through for us."

As they reached the vessel, Lira stood at the helm, a wide grin on her face. "I knew you'd make it! You're tougher than you look," she teased, winking at Ryu.

"Thanks for believing in us," Ryu said, returning her smile. "We really needed a way out."

"Anytime!" Lira replied, gesturing for them to board. "But we've got to hurry. The Executioners won't take this lightly, and they'll be coming for you."

Once aboard, Kaida took the helm while Luna and Zeno secured the sails. "Let's get out of here," she said, her tone serious. "We can regroup and plan our next move once we're safe."

As the ship set sail, Ryu felt a sense of accomplishment wash over him. "We did it, team. We took down Goran and saved Kaida. I couldn't have asked for a better crew."

"Don't forget about me!" Luna interjected playfully. "I'm the one who dealt the final blow."

"True, but we all played our part," Theo added, leaning against the railing. "It's our teamwork that makes us strong."

"I'm just glad we're all back together," Zeno said, a hint of relief in his voice. "But we need to stay alert. The Executioners will come after us, and we have to be ready."

As they sailed into the horizon, the sun began to dip below the waves, painting the sky in hues of orange and pink. The crew stood together, united by their triumph but aware of the challenges that lay ahead.

"Next stop," Ryu said, gazing out at the open sea, "Is finding the rest of our friends and taking down the Executioners once and for all."

Lira nodded, her eyes sparkling with determination. "Let's do this. I'm in for the long haul."

With renewed vigor and a sense of purpose, the crew sailed forward into the unknown, ready to face whatever challenges awaited them on their journey to freedom.

As the ship sailed smoothly across the waves, the atmosphere buzzed with anticipation. Suddenly, Lira stepped forward, her stance confident but her expression playful. "Alright, everyone, I think it's time for a little surprise!"

With a dramatic flourish, she pulled off a carefully placed wig and disguise, revealing the familiar face of Franky. "Surprise! It's me, Franky!" he announced, a wide grin spreading across his face.

The crew erupted in laughter, Ryu shaking his head in disbelief. "Franky! You had us worried there for a second! We thought we lost you back on the island!"

"Yeah! What a way to make an entrance!" Kaida added, chuckling. "But seriously, what's with the disguise?"

"I had to blend in, didn't I?" Franky replied, striking a pose. "But I've got some serious advice for you all. Listen up! You guys shouldn't be heading to the Executioners' headquarters right now."

"Why not?" Luna asked, her brow furrowing. "We just took down Goran. We should capitalize on our momentum!"

Franky shook his head vigorously. "No, no, no! They're gonna be on high alert now. If we show up there, we'll be walking right into a trap. Trust me, I've seen enough action to know when it's time to regroup!"

Zeno nodded, his expression thoughtful. "He's got a point. We've just drawn attention to ourselves, and heading straight for their base could be disastrous."

"I agree," Ryu added, crossing his arms. "We need to be strategic about this. We can't afford to lose anyone else."

"What do you suggest we do instead?" Theo asked, leaning forward. "We can't just sit here and do nothing."

Franky's eyes lit up as he contemplated their next move. "How about we head for Maximum Line Island? It's a hub of trade and activity, and it's far enough away from the Executioners' headquarters. We can gather information, regroup, and plan our next steps."

Kaida considered the proposal. "That could work. We might even find some new allies or resources there."

Luna nodded enthusiastically. "Plus, it'll give us time to recuperate and make sure everyone's okay after the fight."

"Exactly!" Franky exclaimed, clapping his hands together. "And who knows? Maybe there's some crazy tech or inventions we can get our hands on while we're there!"

Ryu smiled, the prospect of new adventures igniting a spark in his eyes. "Alright, Maximum Line Island it is! Let's set a course!"

As Kaida adjusted the ship's heading, the crew began to chatter excitedly about their upcoming journey. Franky leaned against the railing, a satisfied grin on his face. "Just think of all the possibilities! We might even find a way to upgrade our ship while we're there!"

Theo raised an eyebrow. "What do you have in mind? You know I'm always up for some upgrades!"

"Just wait until you see my latest designs!" Franky said, his enthusiasm infectious. "I've been working on some new tech that will blow your mind!"

As the ship sailed toward Maximum Line Island, the crew felt a renewed sense of purpose. They were more than just a group of friends; they were a family ready to take on whatever challenges lay ahead.

"Let's make this a journey to remember!" Ryu shouted, raising a fist in the air. "For our fallen friends, and for the future we'll create together!"

With their spirits high and determination set, they sailed off into the sunset, ready to embrace the unknown and forge new paths in their quest for freedom and justice.